# The Devil's Dozen

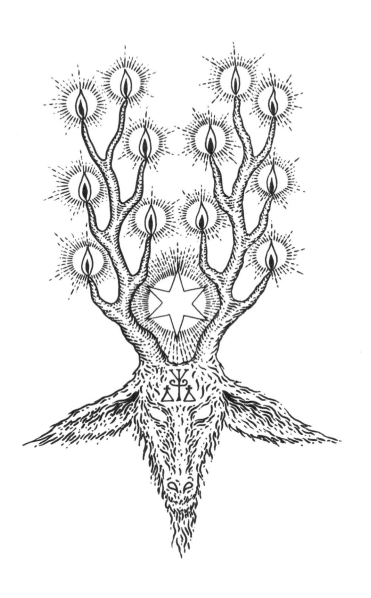

# The Devil's Dozen
## *Thirteen Craft Rites of the Old One*

by
**Gemma Gary**

With line illustrations by the author
and photography by Jane Cox

First North American Edition, 2020
First Printing, 2020
ISBN 978-0-7387-6570-9

Originally published by Troy Books Inc. 2015
ISBN 978-1-909602-19-9

Llewellyn Publications is a registered trademark of Llewellyn Worldwide Ltd.

**Cataloging-in-Publication Programme data  is on file with the British National Bibliography.**

Llewellyn Publications
A Division of Llewellyn Worldwide Ltd. 2143 Wooddale Drive
Woodbury, MN 55125-2989 www.llewellyn.com

Printed in the United States of America

For the Fellows of
Ros an Bucca
and with thanks for their kind
participation in the imagery for this
book

# Contents

Photographs by Jane Cox between pages 80 - 81

# Introduction

The historical creature that is the witch is one who has, by tradition, long been held to have gained useful access to unseen powers and arcane wisdom via contact with the hidden world of spirit; initiated via compact and conference with an entity – mysterious, powerful, 'supernatural' and 'uncanny' in nature. This presence, deeply permeating the historical lore of the witch, is sometimes identified as the familiar spirit, the Fae Folk or even the King of the Faery. Most often however, he is revealed to be the 'Devil' himself. His chosen form may be that of man, yet of animal also, or a mixed, therianthropic manifestation.

# THE DEVIL'S DOZEN

Distinction and separation between the familiar spirit, the Fae, the Devil, and indeed the witch, is not as clean-cut as it might at first be perceived. For the 'old style' witch, the Devil is the initiator and awakener of power, vision and wisdom, and the revealer of the witch's path; that which deviates from the restrictive and normative ways of 'civilised' folk. The old Devil of the witches is the very rend in the veil betwixt the worlds, an embodiment of the power and spirit of witchcraft itself.

Distinct, however, is the witches' 'Devil' from the popular concept of 'Satan' as the very embodiment and actuator of all evil. The Church itself, and the normative society constructed around it, upheld a perverse ideology of the moral virtuousness of suffering, poverty and subjugated fear of a terrible, jealous and vengeful god created in their image. The Devil, however, presided over the supposed 'evils' of personal power, freedom, sexual pleasure, dancing, feasting, ecstatic celebration and all things joyous. The witch however, may discern in this figure the 'dark' and 'earthy' half of the divine, divorced and stripped away from Godhead by the Church and given a separate identity.

Whilst the survival into the present day of a 'pagan cult of the horned god', guarded and kindled by witches, and totally uninfluenced by centuries of Christian and Church domination, is a highly unlikely thing, something of his spirit and presence would appear to have lingered in regional faery lore, seasonal custom and folk tradition. Yet, ironically, it may perhaps be the Church, in its keenness to eradicate adherence to pagan divinity by grafting and projecting it onto the diabolical, that has, unwittingly, most thoroughly preserved the potency, liberation and illumination of the 'Old One' and handed him back to the witches as the 'Devil'.

A bearer of forbidden gifts was he; possessed of the ability to bestow power upon those who dared to stray from the conforming flock and enter upon his hidden path. In rejecting normative restriction, helplessness and impotence, the powers of the old way of the Devil offered the possibility to seize some control over one's own life and fate and to divert the course of circumstance in accordance with one's own will.

Unto ailment could cures be brought, exorcism unto ill fortune and ill influence, fulfilment unto the desires of love, and destruction unto the oppressive, abusive and the cruel. Unto the state of poverty could some alleviation be brought, particularly via the ready willingness of others to part with coin for the employment of those possessed of arcane powers, wisdom and vision via their dealings and compacts with the world of spirit.

The old rites, ways and means via which one might enter into compact with the Old One, the spirits and otherworldly power, have, unto the eyes of the Church, the appearance of desecration and diabolic renunciation of good for the forces of evil. Unto the eyes of the 'old style' witch however, such rites are nothing more than a rejection of Church dogma, guilt and control for the Devil's path of power.

# INTRODUCTION

Subjugation unto repressive concepts of divinity having been rejected, the witch and worker of magic entered into a close, working relationship and union with the Old One and the ancient power and compassion of the world of spirit. Unto the witch and the traditional worker of magic, the Church however was also home to much useful power in the way of curing, cursing, protection, exorcism and blasting, and so the ways of the Church were not rejected entirely. It was instead the mediating control by the clergy or priesthood of such powers and traditional magic that were shunned by the operative practitioner.

Centuries of witch tradition would however appear to have been discarded and denied by many of today's neo-pagan witches, who insist that their worship and concept of the old gods survives in an intact and uninfluenced pre-Christian form. Any suggestion that our horned god has any relation to the old Devil is commonly met with a reaction of complete horror and utter denial, as is the suggestion that the traditional artes of the witch are inclusive of the ability to work baneful magic, despite all that history records.

Such rejections are, I feel, a denial of much of the old potency of witchcraft, and those things that most garnered a useful fear and respect for its artes, and create instead a respectable, tolerated and passive 'New Age' eccentricity.

Passiveness has also sadly been the fate of the Old One within the rites and ways of much that is neo-pagan witchcraft; his traditional 'darker' aspects are an uncomfortable inconvenience to be ignored in favour of his entirely green and benign role as subordinate consort to the goddess.

Witch tradition and the witches' god in his darker aspects have not been discarded entirely, for they are nurtured within various rarefied streams and branches of the Craft to which the Old One is central. This is not to say that there is any rejection, or subordination of the witches' goddess within such streams; far from it, for it is through the Old One, as guardian of the threshold betwixt the Ways, that the deeper mysteries of Our Lady, the progenitrix, may be approached. Unto her also shall a book of devotion be made manifest.

Within such Craft streams, the 'Devil' or the 'Old One' remains as the old initiator; the opener of the 'Way Betwixt', and the awakener of the spirit of the witch unto the crooked path of vision, illumination and power.

He remains as the psychopomp leader of the Wild Hunt; the primal spirit horde, going forth at the parting of the veil, across the twilight landscape, chasing death into life and life into death.

With the waxing and waning of the year he remains also as the old spirit of the land; his guise ever shifting from the foliate verdant mask to the white skull of death's tide. In hedge, hill, wood and heath he remains the innate and haunting presence of the wild and lonely places.

His presence remains in the old witch-rites; perhaps invoked into corporeal reality via the body of the Magister of the companie, a role often bearing the title 'Devil', a mediating vessel guised by mask, horns and hides.

Manifestation and phenomena of his presence are evoked also, by the solitary practitioner and assembled companie alike, upon or around physical representations such as the skull, the cleft staff and the stone. These representations and fetishes of the Old One may bear fire, by candle or torch, from which the witch may kindle their own tapers within devotional rites in honour of the Old One as the bestower and awakener of the light of 'All Wisdom' and mystic illumination.

Within the lore and shifting forms of the witches' Devil may we find Lucifer the light bearer, the hunters betwixt the worlds – Herne, Odin and Woden, the Otherworld Faery King, antecessor of the Wise – Cain; born of Eve and the Serpent Lucifer, and the fiery Old Goat Azazel is he.

Here, within these pages, shall be given thirteen Craft rites of the Old One; rites of vision, sacred compact, dedication, initiation, consecration, empowerment, protection, illumination, union, transformation and devotion. They make no claim to historicity; some draw forth from the rich lore of witchcraft's long history, whilst others draw from the rites and ways of what has come to be known as 'modern traditional witchcraft' and from 'Old Craft'. Yet they are my own creations all; given in hope that they may provide usefulness or inspiration, and each a personal offering of devotion unto the starlit and smoking altar of the Old One.

Gemma Gary
Boscastle and St Buryan, November 2014

# The Man In Black
## *The Witch's Compact*

**T**hroughout the long, winding and not entirely penetrable way that is witchcraft's strange history, one figure, equally enigmatic, is repeatedly encountered. He appears, often unexpectedly by tradition, at the moment of inception between the witch's leaving of the path of ordinary life, to cross the threshold unto the crooked path of the Wise. It is the 'Dark Man' or the 'Man in Black' who guides the witch across this threshold upon the path of Return, which is the path away from the established order of 'the world of men', back via the way of the wild and the 'Other' unto reunion with the company of spirit, power and the primal source of 'All'.

It is fitting that the witch's guide back unto the 'wild side' is often accompanied by animals, or, true to his liminal nature, he may appear in the form of these animals, usually black, such as a hound, bull, goat or crows being amongst many of his chosen bestial forms. All inversions and reversals of Man's 'normalities' are his ways. Black is the form of the guide unto the night-side of the world of spirits and 'Otherness', but black also is the mask and guise of the deliverer unto the way of power and wisdom; for in truth he is the bearer of the hidden light.

Witch history indicates to us that his initial appearance unto the unrealised witch occurs most often under certain circumstance; suddenly and unexpectedly during the performance of repetitive tasks, or when journeying on foot, alone from one place to another, both being activities conducive to a 'day-dreamy' trance-like, meditative state, or deep thought and contemplation. Moments of despair and desperation, which in themselves can be pivotal times of life-change and momentous decision making, and thus very much liminal in nature, have also been the catalyst for his manifestation; bringing assuagement and aid unto the troubled witch.

# THE MAN IN BLACK

Alongside these common patterns, history also teaches us that the appearance of the Man in Black may indeed occur at any time, and may even be intentionally initiated by the witch by means of ritual conjuration, or by mere desire.

## A Call Unto the 'Dark Man'

Unto the aspirant who desires to cross the threshold to the old way of the witch, or unto the witch who, in a time of need, seeks the aid of the Old One, or to renew their compact upon the path of Return; I offer the following rite.

Set forth, alone, to some secret and special place away from the intrusion of human activities and prying eyes. This journey, on foot, must be undertaken as a meditative act in itself, and one must be acutely open to any signs, omens or uncanny presences, subtle or not so, that may present themselves in the landscape through which you pass. This must be so, for it is known that once one has made the decision to call upon him, the Dark

Man may choose to pre-empt any ritual or conjuration by making an appearance, before such an act can be attempted, in either human or bestial form.

When the secret place has been reached, a circle, or working ring, must in some manner be marked upon the ground, be it inscribed in the earth, set out by a good length of cord, marked by chalk, or by any other means. The ring must be large enough to encompass a space within which one can both kneel down, and circumnambulate about a small central fire.

There, build and light the fire, and begin a slow, backward pace about it in the direction against the sun; the journey to the left, until the Lord's Prayer has thrice been spoken backwards:

*Nema.*
*Reve dna reve rof,*
*yrolg eht dna, rewop eht, modgnik eht si eniht rof,*
*Live morf su reviled tub, noitatpmet otni ton su dael dna.*
*Su tsniaga ssapsert taht meht evigrof ew sa,*

*sessapsert ruo su evigrof dna.*
*Daerb yliad ruo yad siht su evig.*
*Nevaeh ni si ti sa, htrea ni enod eb lliw yth.*
*Emoc modgnik yht.*
*Eman yht eb dewollah,*
*nevaeh ni tra hcihw,*
*rehtaf ruo.*

Upon the completion of this, kneel in genuflection before the fire, facing the north, and, using the left hand, cast into the flames a handful of elder, thistle and mugwort. Into the rising smoke speak these words:

*Here encompassed at the Cross of the Ways,*
*upborne upon the fire of my Will,*
*out into evenfall's gloam my call and spell;*
*O Dark One, Intecessor, Robin, Old Janicot!*
*Deliver Me!*
*I call for thy visitation as of old,*
*by vision, dream or manifest form,*
*come thou!*
*By guise of man, dark-hooded or hatted,*
*by hound, or crow, by goat, bull or walking toad;*
*blackened all and bearing light,*

*come thou!*
 *Meet me upon wooded aisle, lonely stile, at*
*thorny hedge or stream's edge,*
*Here or there, now or then,*
*come ye forth!*
*Aid and enjoin me in hallowed compact.*
*From all workers of evil, oppression, slander*
*and deceit deliver me!*
*From all misery and fear save me!*
*For I am a child of the serpent seed.*
*Opener of the hidden and crooked way,*
*set me upon and illumine the path of return;*
*the old path of One and All possibility!*
*My guide and dark companion clad of night,*
*saviour and beacon-light!*
*Deliver me! Deliver me! Deliver me!*

Remain there, waiting, watching, listening, within the circle until the fire has burnt away. The Man in Black's visitation may there occur via his physical presence, in human or bestial guise, or via vision, or some sign manifest in the forms, sounds and movements of the surrounding land. The encounter may occur at another time, at another place, in dream or the waking world, but when and in whatever manner, following the sincere working of this rite, occur it shall.

# Under the Horns
## Dedication & Initiation of the Witch

**F**ollowing the making of the witch's call to encounter and enter into compact with the Old One, the time shall come for the sealing of that compact by the rite of dedication and initiation.

From Somerset to Scotland, one setting for such a rite, encountered again and again within witch tradition and lore, is the churchyard. It is a surprise to some that the old churches and the grounds they stand in are old friends of the witch; as places where folk come together to contemplate and commune with the divine, where rites of union, blessing, exorcism and of the dead are conducted and where the power and presence of God, the Angles and the Saints are invoked, they are places of immense use to the rites and magic of the witch. A sacred place is a powerful place, and the 'old style' witch will have their own unique ways of working at such places regardless of the fact that they perceive and interact with the divine and the spiritual differently to those who more usually attend them. As locations for spiritual interaction, churches are quite naturally 'places betwixt' where the 'Otherworld' and its presences may be particularly palpable.

The churchyard, as a burial ground, is a particularly potent 'place betwixt' and thus highly useful to the witch; the graves being employable within traditional charms and rites of 'get rid of' magic, healing, protection and turning. Their dust or earth have their old uses within curative charms, acts of blessing and of cursing. As the centre of a web of 'corpse roads' and 'spirit paths', converging from across the landscape, the churchyard is a place of spirit contact, the sight, and gaining useful information of the past, present and the future. It is to the churchyard the traditionally minded may travel to enter into rites of witch-initiation.

In such circumstances where a candidate is entering into initiation via a witch covine, they might not undertake the rite alone. The candidate may be accompanied by an initiate and guided through the rite which may be performed in the presence of at least some of the covine, and presided over by the Magister or Magistre in the Old One's guise. In this circumstance, the covine will have developed their own way of carrying out each of the rite's particulars, with certain actions being administered by the presiding witch in the role of the Old One. The rite here given however, is described for solitary use but is easily adaptable for group situations.

Solitary initiation, it must be remembered, is not self initiation. At a successful rite of witch-initiation, one is never alone for true initiation is a transformative process of death, rebirth and illumination, imparted by numen and spirit presences.

Secrecy and stealth is of course important in all witch-rites and magical workings, but all the more so when working in churchyards because of the obvious suspicions and negative preconceptions that will be aroused if attention were drawn to such activities. A remote churchyard, or one that is in a naturally quiet setting will be most suitable, and the timing and weather conditions will be allies in ensuring that the rite goes unobserved by unwelcome corporeal human eyes. A mist or fog shrouded night will conceal your activities, and a wet or stormy night will naturally keep most late night walkers indoors.

## A Rite of Witch-Initiation & Dedication

At midnight, at the full of the moon, go to the churchyard bearing with you a hooded cloak, a candle lantern, a sharp and clean knife for use in the arte, a good bottle of drink and a small vessel of oil or grease mixed with soot. Have with you also a cord with which to mark out a circle large enough for you to kneel within with your other items.

When you have entered quietly through the gate, stop, and without words acknowledge the spirit wards of the churchyard and affirm the nature of your business there; for they must be assured you have not arrived to work damage or harm to the place they guard, but have come for a sacred purpose. One can also ask the spirit wards of a churchyard for aid in keeping one's work hidden from prying eyes.

Go to the north side of the church, and there mark out your circle and arrange the things you have brought with you. Remove your clothing and wrap yourself within your hooded cloak. Light the candle in your lantern and begin the circumambulation. Backwards, and in the direction against the sun, slowly walk around the outside of the church. This is to be a contemplative act, in which one is walking the 'path of return' away from the ways of ordinary man and his separation from nature, the wild and the 'other', to tread the path of the witch, back into the shadows to find that hidden light and re-union with the divine spark from which all proceeds; symbolised this night by the lantern.

To do such a thing in a remote and darkened churchyard is perhaps not an easy task, and spirit presences may arise, taking an interest in your activity, and are likely to arouse fear, as are the mundane sights, sounds and sensations of the night. The mind however must be fixed upon the work, and any fear turned towards fanning the inner fire; setting one's prayers ablaze.

Upon reaching the circle for the ninth time, enter therein and kneel before the light of your lantern and speak, quietly, the following prayer of acceptance:

*On this night and at this hour,*
*Of my own will and accord,*
*The secret Craft, its artes and power*
*I wholly accept by blood and word.*
*By hidden path and backwards Round,*
*By the Devil's lamp revealed,*
*By the toad and the hound,*
*The old pact made and be it sealed.*
*Blackened bull to lead the Wise*
*My call and prayer this night be heard,*
*Spirits of the Way arise,*
*Old One hearken to my word.*
*So Shall it be!*

The right hand is now placed upon the crown of the head, and the left beneath the foot as the dedication is made:

*Old One, Great Initiator,*
*Bearer of the light of All,*
*Illuminator of the Hidden paths of night.*
*I here do pledge all betwixt these my two*
*hands unto thy secret Way,*
*To the curse and blessing of the Wise-Blood*
*aflame!*
*Ever shall I keep the witch's silence,*
*Except it be unto a true brother or sister of*
*the Arte.*
*By blood and word, sealed and bound,*
*Pledged and placed beneath the horns!*
*So shall it be in the Old One's name!*

The knife is now taken up and a small
nick is made to draw forth a little blood,
perhaps from a fingertip, and a drop or
two of blood is allowed to fall upon the
earth. This act is not only an offering of
the self, but the themes of death, rebirth,
and light from the dark are enshrined
within the union of one's life blood with
the earth. Within this initiatory rebirth
is found also the awakening of witch
power, the vehicle and vessel of which is
the witch's blood, and is itself enshrined
within the witch's oneness with the

land and its spiritual reality. The act of blooding has a long history in witch initiation, in which it is cognate with the tradition of the witch's Mark and the sealing of the compact.

In token of this rebirth unto a new life and the Craft, it is fitting that the witch should now take on a new and secret name. In a covine situation, this name would be known only to the witch's brothers and sisters in the arte. The new witch-name is now spoken in the act of anointing, also related to the tradition of the witch's Mark, and the 'Devil's baptism'. It is therefore an act that should be administered by the presiding witch guised in the role of the Old One during a rite of covine initiation.

Take up the pot of soot-mixed grease or oil, and mark the hands and then the brow, the latter in the sign of the six-armed cross, speaking these words:

*In the Old One's name,*
*Be I (name),*
*Marked and anointed as Wise One and witch.*
*So Shall it be!*

It is at this point that the witch might choose to dedicate some of the working items of the arte, such as the knife and perhaps a staff or wand. In group situations the tools might now be presented and dedicated to their purpose before the covine. The item is taken up and held above the lantern with these words:

*By the spirits of the Way,*
*And in the Old One's name,*
*I dedicate this my blade of Craft and Arte.*
*So shall it be!*

The rite is concluded by pouring out some of the drink in offering and thanks to the place, its spirit wards, the spirits of the Hidden Path and the Old One before the witch drinks also.

The items of the rite are carefully gathered up and packed away, and the witch re-dresses to return quietly home to their bed, leaving no visible sign of their activities in the churchyard that night.

# The Witch's Bowl
*Hallowing of the Working Ground*

**W**hether it is for use by a solitary practitioner, or by an assembly of the Craft, a special place will be sought for the working of magic and rites of the Arte. It is essential that such a place is as secluded and as private as is possible, and far from the 'world of men', so as to be a place of wild nature and spirit forces; a place of potency. It is for these reasons that such a place might be referred to as 'the lonely place', 'the secret place', 'the hidden place' or the 'haunted place'.

Where the chosen location possesses also the blessing of remoteness, journeys to visit the working ground will embody an act of magical and sacred pilgrimage. Journeying and wandering in this manner is, for the witch, a meditative and power gathering act so useful to the rites and workings of the Arte. The chosen place will also be perceived to be possessed of some special or uncanny virtue, spirit presences, and natural potency, and thus described by some as 'pulse spots'. Such virtues are of course highly useful to the work of the witch, and places with a proximity to water are highly regarded for their liminal quality, whereby the Otherworldly may be all the more accessible.

The Wise will visit the potential working ground upon numerous occasions, there entering into exploration via contemplation and meditation, to imbibe of and engage with the spirit and essence of the place through all of the senses. Signs that a suitable place has indeed been found may take the form of the location arising in one's dreams, indicating perhaps that a deeper, working interaction is being invited.

The working ground having been positively identified, a rite may be performed in order to set the ground 'apart' and dedicate and empower the place unto its new purpose. Such a rite may also serve to forge and seal the working relationship between the Wise and the spirit of place.

# THE WITCH'S NOWL

Central to the rite here given for this purpose is the witch's nowl; a large nail of iron employed by some practitioners and lineages of the Craft. The witch's nowl is associated primarily with power and potency; such associations arising quite naturally from its form and the substance from which it is created. The form of the nowl is of obvious phallic nature with its attendant virtues of fertility and life giving force. Akin to the knife, the pin and the thorn, its use in magic often employs the nowl's ability to penetrate and to fix in order to convey and impart the intent and power of the spell or rite, and give life and fertility to the working. Its substance, being of iron, has its old associations with power, blood and with fire; telluric and heavenly. The Nowl within witch rites, along with other items forged of iron, is regarded also as deeply emblematic of Old Tubal Cain; the 'Hairy One', born of the 'Serpent Blood', the first smith and bearer of Craft, skill and power.

It is a tradition found within some lineages of the Craft that a potent fire, often depicted as a serpent, dwells within the earth, animating and empowering the land with life. This fire flows also within the body of the witch as the 'Serpent Blood' and is itself of the Divine Fire which fell to earth from the heavens. Witch-blood, the bloodline of the Serpent, is said to have been initiated by primordial union between man and the Old Ones, the bearers of light, thus is the mystic fire often depicted betwixt the horns of the Horned One; the awakener, illuminator and forefather of the witch.

It is this Serpent Fire which shall be employed within the rite here given via the use of the witch's nowl. Within acts of operative witchcraft and cunning, the nail is often pushed or struck into the ground for various purposes. As Steve Patterson, a witch and traditional magician in Cornwall explains, the iron nail may be used to 'pin down' your magic onto the land, and Cecil Williamson spoke of witches putting a nail to the ground in graveyards in order to listen to the spirits of the departed.

Another item employed within the rite here given is the 'Devil's Scourge'. Within some traditions and lineages, this scourge has horse hair in place of the leather or silken thongs more often encountered in some expressions of the Craft. To many Crafters, the horse represents not only witch-divinity in both its male and female aspects, but a symbolic vehicle for magical power and force itself. It is for these associations that items relating to horses are to be found employed as magical and ritual tools within some Craft circles. Such items of course often relate to the tame or harnessed horse, and so symbolise the harnessing of power unto the will of the witch, and its conjuring into, or sending forth from the witch's circle.

The nail of course is also part of the magical symbolism of the horse, harnessed and shod. This symbolism is exemplified in the practice, found in some Craft traditions, of 'shodding the stang' whereby a nail may be ritually struck into the base end of the stang; the forked staff, sometimes called 'the

Horse', representing the presence of the divine and Otherworldly power within the circle. Thrust into the earth, the nail within the stang's base represents the fallen telluric fire below to be drawn upon to empower the magical rites and workings of witchcraft.

Reified within the form of the 'Devil's Scourge' is the Serpent, thus it is a tool emblematic of telluric potency, as well as witch-power and divine force. Snake and scourge alike being also phallic in form, it too is emblematic of fertility and enlivenment. Like the iron of the nail, the fiery scourge is also exorcising and punishing in nature and so has its place within rites of banishing and blasting.

Within the empowering of the working ground however, the 'Devil's Scourge' may be employed to ritually and symbolically 'strike' the ground in order to stir and raise the Serpent Fire of the land, to conjure forth the 'steed of power' into the circle, and to impart fertility and potency to all magical and ritual acts performed therein. Within a rite of assembled Crafters, the scourge would be employed by the presiding witch in the role of the Old One, yet is of use also to the solitary practitioner. Again, the rite here given should easily be adaptable for both circumstances.

## 𝕬 𝕽ite of 𝕳allowing for the 𝖂orking 𝕲round

Required for this rite are the following: A large nail of iron, an iron knife or a staff of blackthorn, some means of marking out the circle and of making a fire, the horse hair scourge, a cup or horn, a good drink, an incense containing dragon's blood resin, some charcoal and a suitable vessel to burn it in.

The walk to the secret place should be a silent, meditative act; breathing and drawing deeply of the spirit essence of the land as the rite's participants go.

Upon reaching the place, one should begin by quietly clearing the earth that is to form the area of the working ground, before visibly marking out the circumference of the circle, and go about gathering wood for a small fire. Again, these should be meditative acts in which the spirits of place are acknowledged and silently called upon. The gathered wood is placed, for the time being, with the items for the rite in the east, where the lighted lantern burns and the incense smoke arises from the coals.

The iron knife, or blackthorn staff, is now taken up, and is used to trace the circle's edge, sun-wise from the east and back to the east three times whilst a charm is spoken:

> *Thrice be conjured Compass Round,*
> *Devil's Acre, Dancing Ground,*
> *Marked and hallowed Castle moat,*
> *Blessed field of the goat!*
> *Meadow of the Hidden Flame,*
> *Hallowed in the Horned One's Name!*

The knife or blackthorn staff is then used to mark the equal-armed cross in the centre of the circle; its four arms aligned to the four cardinal points. About this sign, in stillness and silence, those assembled now breath and imbibe deeply of the spirit presences and essences of the place in inner communion, so as to become one with the physical and spiritual reality of the locus.

The iron nowl is now brought to the centre of the circle, and held aloft to the heavens in the right hand. Within a covine rite, this is done by the company together. As the nowl is held, a charm is spoken to draw down the divine fire from the heavens above:

*Horned Father of the Wise,*
*Serpent-fire of the skies,*
*Let fall to earth that ancient flame,*
*Azazel, Tubal-Qayin!*
*By thunderbolt and starry shower,*
*To tend and turn the Horse of Power!*

When the nowl is felt to burn bright with the fire of the heavens, it is switched to the left hand and brought down to the cross marked upon the earth, and pushed or struck deep into its midst. Within this act is reified the bringing of the spiritual light into matter and manifestation, and

the union of spirit with the elements of
the manifest world.

*Dark Bull of the coal-black ground,*
*Hallowed of the witches' Round,*
*Stir the serpent of the deep,*
*Arise earth's fire to our keep.*
*Set the fertile plot ablaze,*
*To turn the mill and work the maze.*

With these words having been spoken
in preparation, the small fire is now to
be built upon the cross and lit, and the
Devil's Scourge is taken up in the right
hand. A sun-wise mill dance is now begun
about the fire, the earth symbolically and
rhythmically scourged to raise the serpent
of the earth, bring fertility unto the rite
and to drive the 'steed of power' onward.
During the mill dance, a charm is used,
such as the following. After a while, the
charm may develop into a chant using
the last two lines only:

*Serpent turn, awake, arise,*
*About the fire the Mill be trod,*
*Enflame the Circle of the Wise,*

*By scourge, by broom, by dancing rod.*
*By Cauldron-cup and iron blade,*
*Tread the mill about the fire,*
*By Serpent-seed and powers bade,*
*Stir and raise the Serpent higher!*

When the potency of the inner fire and that of the working ground are felt to have been raised to a high intensity, the participants are to drop to their hands and knees in order to give the raised power unto the encompassed earth. After a little while, the cup is filled and brought, with the iron knife, to the centre of the working ground. Held above the fire, the knife blade is lowered into the cup and its content blessed:

*By the Old Serpent's fire, above and below,*
*By the quarters crossed where All is One!*
*Hallowed and blessed,*
*So shall it be!*

A little of the cup's content is poured into the fire before the participants of the rite partake. The rite is now closed by the cup being carried around the circle's edge against the sun, from east back to east, pouring a little drink upon the earth at each of the cardinal points. The circle may be opened by being traced, as it was before with the blade or staff, but against the sun. All is now cleared away, and the place departed with no visible signs of the rite being left. After three days and three nights, the nowl is retrieved from the earth at the working ground's midst.

# Raising the Stang

**F**rom certain branches of the Craft, the stang has arisen to such prominence as to arguably have become a prime cultic emblem of 'modern traditional witchcraft', in perhaps the way the pentacle or the athame have become emblematic tools of the Wica.

The origins of the stang of the witches, and its point of entry into the Craft cannot be stated with any great certainty, and so will perhaps forever be the subject of mystery and debate. The 'stang', as a witches' ritual 'pole', topped with two or more tines, is of a form recognisable in many 'woodcuts' and other old depictions of witcherie, in which a forked pole object may be seen employed by witches in various magical or ritual acts.

Numerous forked wooden implements have their varied uses within folk-magical and cunning practice; for ritualistic, divinatory and operative magical purposes.

# THE DEVIL'S DOZEN

The stick or staff is anciently depicted in the possession of witches, magicians, Cunning men and Wise women, but it is, however, cognate with the wand, and thus a traditional magician's hand-tool of both ritual and operative magic; for the conjuring of spirits, the raising and directing of powers, the drawing of magical circles, the banishing of evil and the blasting of wrongdoers.

The stang however, as employed in many branches of the Craft, is not a hand-tool of operative practice, but an item of pure ritual symbolism. Within such usage, the witches' stang is a consecrated and hallowed item of power which is stood within the ground, either at the circle's centre, or at its edge. It is for this reason that some branches of the Craft 'shod' their stang with one or more iron nails to prevent the power within it from draining out into the earth; following the old tradition  that spirits and magical power cannot cross a barrier of iron. Iron is itself seen, however, as a potent magical tool which, according to usage and intent, can be used to direct and impart magical influences as well as acting as a barrier to halt them. Thus the act of 'shodding the stang' is made with the appropriate intent, mindful of the directional nail pointing upward into the shaft of the stang, and therefore a barrier to any downward draining flow of power. To do such a thing however to the wand or conjuring stick/staff would not be desirable, for it is its purpose within many magical workings to allow power to flow through it, or to be directed from it. Whilst both may be forked and share some symbolism, the conjuring stick and the stang are quite distinct in their uses.

Foremost, the stang may be said to be an image of the Old Horned One; the tines of the fork of course being cognate with the horns, and an altar of the Mysteries. As a representation of the Old One, it is not merely an image, but a charged vessel, for the power raised and stored within it is that of the Old One himself, and it is at the stang that the manifest presence of the old witch-god is called forth.

In form, the witches' stang is often the traditional pitchfork; with its shaft of ash, that most magical of trees, and topped with two or more tines of iron. This is of course a most fitting representation of the old witch-god, for its hand forged iron-work we may see as evocative of the old blacksmith; the witch-god as Tubal Cain, and the knowledge of the artes of agriculture and husbandry of the land given by the Old One unto man. In magical thought, iron is also a manifestation of the telluric fire, and the stang is also seen in some branches of the Craft as the Old Serpent of the earth, raised and forked of tongue, to pour forth its power unto the circle of the Wise.

The ritual shodding of the stang is an act further emblematic of the old smith, the tradition of the stang as the horse, the fire of creation/gnosis fallen from the heavens and the serpentine telluric fire – thus in the shodding are the worlds above and below united.

As both a representation of the witch-god, and an altar, the stang is often set to stand at the northern edge of the circle; a direction often regarded in 'Old Craft' circles as a portal or gateway to the numinous, spirit presences and the otherworldly. So placed, the stang is representative of the witch-god as keeper of the way between the worlds; the psychopomp guide of the witch going forth, and of otherworldly virtues and presences entering into the circle or arte. As 'the horse' the stang represents the vehicle of power and spirit ingress and egress; the bearer of spirit forces and divine presence, cognate with the lore of the wild hunt and the horse as bearer of the witch god and wild hunter, chasing spirits between the worlds. As a vehicle of spirit, and opener of the ways to the death mysteries, the stang is also the initiatic tree of sacrifice; the tau cross.

Although a prime Craft symbol of the old witch-god, the stang stands in union betwixt the female and male mysteries within those traditions that set female symbols to the left of the stang, such as the cup or horn, and the male symbols to the right such as the iron blade. In union of these dualities, the stang may represent either, or both, the divine androgyne and the divine 'child of light'. The Old One is himself a god of duality; reflected throughout the seasonal cyclic tides of light, and dark, waxing and waning, life and death, via which each of his faces is revealed. Further dualities are brought into union in the stang stood within the ground; heaven and earth, the physical and the spiritual, 'as above, so below'. The theme of duality and its uniting is potently depicted in the 'horns' of the twain-forked stang, united at the single shaft. Here, at this point of mystic union, the lantern or candle is sometimes affixed; emblematic of the light of 'All wisdom' arising from the realising of 'One Pointedness' or that 'All is One'.

## The Rites of Hallowing, Shodding & Raising the Stang

Required for this rite are a vessel to hold the fire, the pentacle of arte or the stone, a cauldron of water, a vessel of coals to burn incense or a bundle of empowering herbs such as mugwort, a hammer, a good iron nail and a Compass-plotting cord. Have also the human skull and two long bones, or carved representations of such, along with the sword, broom, knife and horn/cup of the companie, and some good drink. Have also a candle for each participant, the lantern and an aspergillum of horsehair or herbs prepared.

Central to the rites of the stang is the theme of unity, thus it will be found embodied within each stage of the rites, beginning with the preparations. Together, as a meditative act of unity, the participants of the rite shall prepare the working ground; carefully clearing the space of debris and gathering the fuel for the fire.

The companie's new stang, being the focus of our operations, shall be stood within the earth to establish the centre of the working ground, and employed to mark a perfect circle. Around its base shall be the looped end of the Compass-plotting cord, which shall be half the length of the desired diameter of the Circle; such as a 4' 6" cord to create the traditional 9' witch's Circle. The other end of the cord, being pulled taut, will allow the plotting out of the Circle's edge, by such means as inscription in the earth with a staff, knife or sword, or by leaving an encompassing trail of a substance such as ashes or chalk. One may also lay down another length of cord or even an iron chain to form other traditional markers of the Circle's physicality. Following the plotting of the Compass, the stang is withdrawn from the ground to held be in the Magister's keeping.

Place at the eastern edge of the Compass the fire vessel, the lantern and the knife. At the southern edge place the stone or pentacle of arte. At the west place the cauldron of water, the aspergillum and the drink-filled cup. At the north, place the skull and bones. The 'bridge' shall be fashioned by sword and broom at the north-eastern edge, with the censer of incense or the bundle of smoking herbs. The companie are now ready to enter the working ground, via the 'bridge', and led by the Magister of the rite bearing the stang. The broom and censer/herbs may now be placed with the skull in the north, and the sword in the east with the fire and knife.

The Magister takes his position at the centre of the circle, as others of the companie work to exorcise the working ground and to conjure the compass by the methods preferred, perhaps by those previously given within this book. The spirits and virtues of the cross-quarters are now called forth so that the Compass may be blessed, thus also those assembled within it, by the lantern, the stone or pentacle of arte, the casting of waters from the aspergillium, and the smoke of the incense or herbs; each taken thrice about the circle in the direction of the sun.

The Magister shall now call forth the presence of the Old One, and the spirits, to converge upon the stang at the crossing of the Ways. He strikes the stang thrice upon the ground and (using the prefferred god-name of the companie) gives the conjuration:

*Bucca, Bucca, Bucca!*
*Ward and farer of the Path*
*revealer of the ways of night*
*Come by fire, Forge and Hearth*
*Come ye bearer of the Light!*
*About the stang are dances trod*
*By stone by bone and rising smoke*
*Come ye forth O witches' god*
*Unto the stang we thee invoke!*
*Unto the Castle draw ye near*
*Rend the veil and bridge the Moat*
*Come by skull and horn appear*
*By Ram by Bull by Stag and Goat!*
*Bucca! Bucca! Bucca!*

Upon the striking of the stang to the ground, the assembled companie shall begin a steady mill-dance to gather the spirits and virtues of the Ways and willing the presence of the Old One into the stang throughout the mill as it is held in their midst by the Magister who shall also will that which is gatherd into the body of the stang.

When the powers and presences are felt to have built to sufficient intensity the Magister shall signal the mill to stop by holding the stang aloft, and he shall make the blessing;

*I conjure ye primal spirits and virtues of the Way above;*
*descend and bless our hallowed stang of arte!*
*So shall it be!*

The companie repeat 'so shall it be' and, lowering the stang to the ground, the Magister shall say;

*I conjure ye serpentine spirits*
*and virtues of the way below;*
*arise and bless our hallowed stang of arte!*
*So shall it be!*

The companie repeat 'so shall it be' and the Magister shall take the stang unto the east, there to pass it thrice with the sun through the flames with the words;

*I conjure ye red spirits and virtues of fire;*
*Blaze and bless our hallowed stang of arte!*
*So shall it be!*

The companie repeat 'so shall it be' and the Magister shall take the stang unto the south, and there lay it down and press it firmly upon the pentacle of arte, or knock it thrice with the stone as the words are given:

*I conjure ye white spirits and virtues of earth;*
*Bear and bless our hallowed stang of arte!*
*So shall it be!*

The companie repeat 'so shall it be' and the Magister shall take the stang unto the west, and there take up the waters of the cauldron in his left hand to bathe thrice the body of the stang with the words;

*I conjure ye grey spirits and virtues of water;*
*Bathe and bless our hallowed stang of arte!*
*So shall it be!*

# RAISING THE STANG

The companie repeat 'so shall it be' and the Magister shall take the stang unto the north, and pass it thrice through the rising smoke of the incense, or take up the smoking bundle of wort and three times waft it along the stang's length with the words;

*I conjure ye black spirits and virtues of air;*
*Bellow and bless our hallowed stang of arte!*
*So shall it be!*

The companie repeat 'so shall it be' and the Magister will now return with the stang to the centre of the Compass. Here, the hammer and the nail shall be brought to him so that he, in the role of the Old Blacksmith, may shod the stang by striking the nail into its base with three blows of the hammer. Thus the stang's hallowing is sealed.

Now the Magister shall place the stang to stand in the earth at the circle's midst; the crossing of the Ways, and it shall be prepared by the companie as the true witches' altar. First the skull and bones are brought from the north and arranged at the stang's base; the bones being crossed or open in accordance with time and tide. The lantern and the knife are brought from the east; the lantern set between the 'horns' of the stang, and the knife placed to the right of the skull. From the south, the stone or pentacle of arte is brought and placed before the skull and bones, and the cup of drink is brought from the west and placed to their left.

The altar of the Wise thus prepared, let each now solemnly approach the stang in turn and give reverence in union to the Old One. Let each bear a candle to be lit from the lantern before kneeling in genuflection before the stang. The candles shall be placed about the altar in the form of the six pointed star of union before each shall touch their brow to the earth for a while in silent communion with the Old One before returning to their place in the assembly.

Let now the companie be led by the Magister in a sun-wise mill about the altar so that each, by focus of will and vision, may raise the presences and powers there gathered into greater intensity, and even into phenomenal manifestation.

When the mill is done, let the Magister and the Maid of the rite meet before the stang to hallow by blade and cup the drink, so that all may partake of the night's mystic union betwixt dualities and the self with the divine.

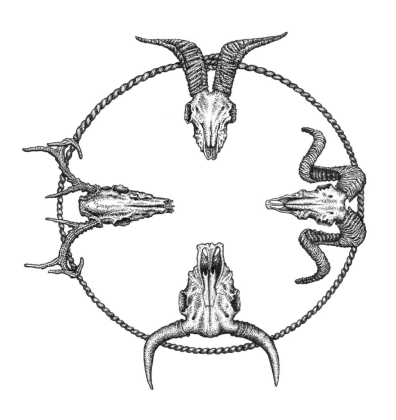

# The Horned Castle
## *A Rite of the Compass*

At either the established and hallowed working ground, or at other locations chosen for various ritual or magical purposes, a ritual conjuration of the witches' Circle, also known in the Craft as the Compass, the Ring, the Castle, or the Blood Acre, is required and will be performed prior to all rites and workings of the Arte. In congruence with the nature of this book, I here give such a rite for the conjuration and consecration of a Circle dedicated unto the Twin Horned One – the Old God of the witches.

The rite of the witches' Compass is a delineation and 'marking out' of the working ground as sacred and separate from mundane space. The Compass is often popularly described as being a space 'between the worlds' for within its bounds may the witches call forth and enjoin in working communion with

Divinity, spirits and magical forces. It is the creation of a place of magical liminality, wherein the old crossways of power are conjured forth.

To the cross-quarter or cardinal directions of the Compass, various manifestations of witch Divinity, spirits and virtues are ascribed by some Craft traditions and lineages. To each are also ascribed certain of the 'workings tools' as well as aspects or purposes of ritual and magic cognate with their nature.

The guardian or warding spirits, the presiding aspects of Divinity and the virtues of each of the cross-quarter Ways are often enshrined, by some traditions and lineages, within various totemic and tutelary animal forms. As is befitting a Compass for the use of dedicants of the Old One, the rite here given describes a Circle whose cardinal directions are ascribed to his traditional horned animal manifestations.

At the Circle's eastern cardinal, the home of the red spirits of fire, we find the ram; the fiery Aries of serpentine horns, and associated with the planetary virtues of Mars. The east is associated with the rising sun and the Spring. It is through the sign of Aries that the sun passes at Spring's arrival. East is of the Old Smith and the forge, and of the awakening and birth of fiery life from the darkness and the depths. East is also the direction of potency, magical power and the fire of the will. Its Craft implements include the knife, the sword, the scourge and the besom of birch.

With the white spirits of the south we find the bull of the earth; the Taurus, before whose sign comes the sun at Midsummer. Associated with the abundant virtues of Venus and the verdant land bathed in the light of the midday sun; life in full fruitful potency and physical, manifest reality are fully illuminated and revealed. Amongst the southern cardinal's Craft implements are the stone, the pentacle, the cross and the platter of food.

Turning to the west, the direction of the grey spirits of water, we find the stag or the old hart. Emblematic of the moon and the Otherworld, the stag or hart is the creature of Gwynn ap Nudd; the Otherworld king of Annwn, and of Herne the Hunter; psychopomp leader of the wild hunt. West is the direction of the Autumnal tide, when the red, fallow and sika deer begin their rutting rituals. West is the direction of the great sea of memory, receiving the sun at the veil of dusk; the liminal time between times and the passing from life into the hidden realms of death. The Craft implements of the west include the cauldron, cup or lunar horn and the mirror.

To the north, we come to the black spirits of air and the dark goat of the Sabbat; the Capricorn through whose sign the sun passes in Winter and associated with the virtues of Saturn. To the witch, north is the direction of midnight; in which all is concealed in invisibility and mystery. North also is the direction for the winds of augury and omen, the voices of spirits, the work of divination and dealings with the realm of the dead. Within the north we may place Craft implements such as the stang, the skull and the smoking censer.

# THE HORNED CASTLE

Encompassed by the ram, the bull, the stag and the goat is the Circle's centre. Here meet the cross-quarter paths of virtue to form the true crossroads; the liminal meeting place at which the virtues conjoin as 'One' and from which they proceed. It is thus the point of 'All possibility', of destruction, transformation and creation. It is for this reason that the cauldron is often set at the Circle's centre, over the fire at the crossing of the Ways.

It will be noticed that the arrangement of the cardinal virtues is quite different to that found more often in popular occult working, in which the opposing relationships run diagonally. The arrangement given here is that which is used by a number of Craft traditions and lineages in which the opposing relationships run crosswise; from ethereal air to corporeal earth, from active fire to receptive water. It is also an arrangement that creates a natural Round; dawn – midday – dusk – midnight, Spring – Summer – Autumn – Winter, birth – living – dieing – death leading on to rebirth and so forth.

# THE DEVIL'S DOZEN

The act of preparing the Circle is in itself an important ritualistic act in which the purposeful placement of the implements is an establishment of, and connection with magical space. The preparation should be conducted with focus and contemplation to assist the opening of the Ways.

The ritual here given may be performed either by a covine or a solitary practitioner, being adapted accordingly.

## A Rite of The Witch's Compass

Let all present be fired with desire, fixed of will and focussed upon the purpose of the rite or working here to be done.

Let the ground be cleared and the Circle's area plotted out, employing the Compass-plotting cord as described in the previous rite. As well as the stang, other items such as the nowl or witch's knife may be pushed into the earth, to establish the centre of the working ground, and to take the looped end of the plotting cord. Whichever devise is employed, the Compass's edge shall now be plotted and delineated as desired; by inscribing the earth with blade or staff, the scattering of substances, or the laying of the Compass cord or chain.

The forked stang or staff is now set to stand at the centre of the working ground, with the skull, a winding horn and a small fire or a lantern arranged at its base. To the east of the circle arrange a pair of ram's horns with the knife or sword, the Devil's Scourge and the besom if it is needed. To the south, have the horns of a bull with the stone, the pentacle or cross and the platter of food. To the west arrange a pair of stag antlers with the cup and the vessel of water. Have there also the cauldron and the mirror if they are needed. To the north of the Circle arrange a pair of goat horns with the censer of incense. In magical or seasonal rites, the central stang may instead be stood at the Circle's edge at the quarter of pertinent virtue, whereby the cauldron may be set up above the central fire. Let each participant have with them a conjuring staff or wand.

# THE DEVIL'S DOZEN

When all is suitably arranged, the Circle is vacated, moving the smoking censer, with cleansing and exorcising herbs cast thereupon, to the north-eastern edge of the Circle; the point between darkness and illumination, death and rebirth. In a covine rite, the sword and broom may be crossed here also.

A moment is now spent in silent contemplation of the place, its spirits and virtue, and the purpose of the night's rite or working. Each participant shall now, in silence enter the Circle, stepping through the rising and purifying smoke, to assemble around the centre as the censer, sword and besom are returned to their places.

The Devil's Scourge is now taken up in the left hand, and the Circle exorcised of all impeding or adverse influences, three times round with symbolic scourging:

*Hekas Hekas Este Bebeloi!*
*By serpent's tongue and lightening strike,*
*Be all hindrance put to flight!*
*By serpent-seed and horse's hoof,*
*Bless the Castle floor to roof!*
*Hekas Hekas Este Bebeloi!*

Let now begin the three-fold casting of the Compass Round. The first is made thrice round by the conjuring staff, the second is made by asperging the Circle's edge thrice round with water drawn from a holy well, in the third the smoking censer is taken thrice round. With each a conjuration is spoken, such as that used within the rite of the Witches' Nowl or the following:

*By ram, by bull, by stag and goat,*
*By water, earth, by smoke and flame,*
*I conjure forth the Castle Moat,*
*Hallowed in the Old One's Name!*
*Thrice be cast O Compass Round,*
*The witches' Mill to turn and spin,*
*Hallowed and horned the working ground,*
*The Circle made, the rite begin!*

The direction in which the conjurations of the Compass are made are, of course, dependant on the nature of the rite or working.

Within the walking of the Circle's Round with the staff, we may find the journey of life. Within the casting of the well waters, we may see the River; the Castle moat separating the world of the living from the world of the dead. Within the bearing round of the smoking censer, we may see the spirit freed from corporeal form in death as well as the eternal fire of the spirit. The chthonic waters of a holy well possess something of the earth, and so its use forms a blessing of the Circle by the elemental virtues of both water and earth, as the use of the censer does so by air and fire. Salt might be added to the water where well water is unobtainable, and the telluric water and the incense and coals may be exorcised ritually by the common formula.

Conjurations are now made at each of the quarters. Beginning at the east, and facing inward to the Circle's centre, take up the conjuring staff and call forth the virtues and powers of the east:

> *I conjure thee,*
> *Red spirits of the forge of dawn,*
> *Great Ram of the East,*
> *Unto the Blood Acre arise!*
> *Guide us on the dancing ground,*

# THE HORNED CASTLE

*Keeper of the Castle's Round,*
*I Conjure thee, I conjure thee, I conjure thee,*
*By horn and hoof so shall it be!*

A conjuration is now made in the same manner at the south of the Circle:

*I conjure thee,*
*White spirits of the noontide earth,*
*Great Bull of the South,*
*Unto the Blood Acre arise!*
*Guide us on the dancing ground,*
*Keeper of the Castle's Round,*
*I Conjure thee, I conjure thee, I conjure thee,*
*By horn and hoof so shall it be!*

The conjuration is now made at the west:

*I conjure thee,*
*Grey spirits of the twilight waters,*
*Great Hart of the West,*
*Unto the Blood Acre arise!*
*Guide us on the dancing ground,*
*Keeper of the Castle's Round,*
*I Conjure thee, I conjure thee, I conjure thee,*
*By horn and hoof so shall it be!*

Lastly, at the north:

*I conjure thee,*
*Black spirits of the midnight winds,*
*Great Goat of the North,*
*Unto the Blood Acre arise!*
*Guide us on the dancing ground,*
*Keeper of the Castle's Round,*
*I Conjure thee, I conjure thee, I conjure thee,*
*By horn and hoof so shall it be!*

At the central fire, the horn is taken up,
and the binding of the spirits and powers
unto the Circle is spoken prior to a call
unto the Old One:

*Horned Castle of the Wise,*
*By the crossroads of the Round,*
*Spirits of the Ways arise!*
*Herein raised and duly bound!*
*So shall it be!*

*Horned One,*
*We bid ye come,*
*Father of the Witches all,*
*by twain-forked staff, by fume and flame,*
*Hearken ye unto our call!*

*Horned One,*
*We bid ye come,*
*Father of the Witches all.*

The horn is now sounded three times and the treading of the Mill is begun about the central fire in the direction against the sun. Throughout this act, all shall earnestly call and pray inwardly unto the Old One, throwing their focus and will fixedly upon the stang and skull, calling there forth the presence of godhead to manifest and give power unto their cause. When the Mill is felt to come to completion, the night's working or rite may now proceed.

# The Wisht Hounds
## Rites of Warding and Turning

The hound or dog, despite its ancient co-evolution and symbiotic relationship with Man, is a creature around which much dark fear exists in superstition and folklore. Such feelings and beliefs, however, arise more probably from Mankind's innate fears surrounding the mysteries of death, the Otherworld and the unknown.

Spectral or feary black hounds abound in British folklore and traditional belief; their apparitions heavily associated with the dusk and midnight haunting of lonely passages, paths, ancient track-ways and crossroads. Lone travellers who have experienced such encounters have reacted with fear at what many interpret as an evil apparition of ill omen, and in particular a portent of death. Such are the beliefs that surround the hound apparitions of the British Isles, including East Anglia's Black Shuck, the Mogah-Doo of Manx tradition, the Barguist in Lancashire and the faery-green Cù Sìth of the Scottish Highlands.

The spirit hound as a harbinger of death pertains to the allied ancient traditions of the Wild Hunt and the Hounds of the Otherworld. As with the lone hound haunting the silent lanes and byways, to catch sight of the Otherworldly pack of the Old Hunter was a foretelling of death's aproach. It is a tradition intimately associated with the mysteries of death and the dead, in which we find the Old One as psychopomp; riding forth to bear away the souls of the dead unto the Otherworld.

As well as chaser of souls, the Otherworldly hound is also widely associated with the role of guardian betwixt the ways; warding the entrance to and from the realm of the dead. This role is reflected also in the tradition of the churchyard Grim; the attendant spirit guardian of the sanctity of old churches and their resting grounds of the dead, often manifesting in the form of a black dog.

*Raising the Stang; the pitchfork stang stands at the circle's centre with the lantern betwixt its tines. The skull & cross-bones, cup, knife and pentacle are arranged at its base.*

*Above and facing; the assembled companie of witches circle the Devil, manifest in a male witch disguised in the 'Grand Array' of animal hides and horns. The burning torches held by the witches are kindled from the Devil's flame; an act of communion with The Old One, his mystic luminosity and the 'witch-fire' within.*

*Above; a male witch as 'The Wild Huntsman' bearing the horn and scourge. Facing; the antlered helmet worn in the rite.*

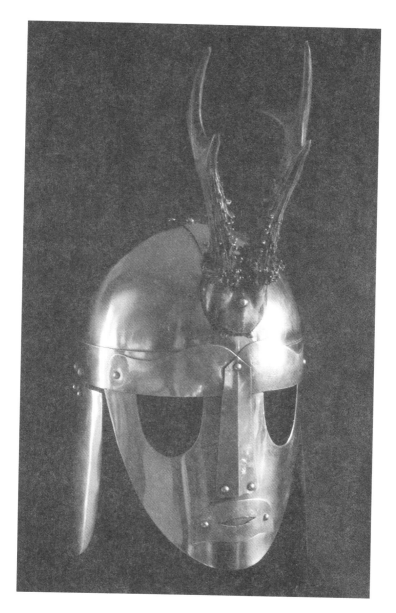

*Therianthropic wood carvings depicting the spirit of 'Otherness' and untamed nature; a ram horned and hooved figure of The Old One carved by Bel Bucca, a 'Deval Sasabonsam' figure and an ithyphallic Pan figure. Author's collection.*

The Museum of Witchcraft and Magic's famous 'Old Hornie', depicting the central figure to many a witches' sabbath; the old goat god, perhaps in the form of a 'guised' witch-master.

*A large and heavy, black painted set of ram's horns said to have been part of a headdress used in the rites of a coven in the Tintagel area in the 1940s. Author's collection.*

This protective influence is also extended to the living. Tradition holds that the lone black spirit hounds, instead of being apparitions of ill omen, may accompany the lonely traveller, guarding, guiding and averting them from harm. One such spiritual guard and guide dog is to be found in Somerset tradition and is known simply as 'The Gurt Dog'. Here, a protective companionship is offered to those walking across the land alone. Such was the faith in the benevolent watchfulness of 'The Gurt Dog' that mothers were happy to leave their children to play on the Quantock Hills, safe in the presence of the spirit hound of Somerset.

The various attributes and associations of the Otherworldly hound are exemplified in the creature's great significance to some traditions, streams and lineages of witchcraft. The ancient concomitance of the hound with the mysteries of death and passage between the realms of the living and the dead, ally the creature to the witches' vital dealings with the Otherworld and the spirits of the dead. Much of the work of the witch deals intimately with liminality, otherness and passage between the worlds, and so the spirit hound, possessed of the ability to float through the air, pass through walls and dense hedges, to become invisible and walk with the dead, make the spirit hound emblematic of such virtues, whilst the traditional haunts of the black hound, and its appearances at the betwixt times of dusk and midnight serve to affirm the creature's liminal nature. With the spirit hound, the witch will also associate the tides, passage and powers of the moon, as well as the sanctity, spirits and virtues of place. With the Old One the spirit hound is also heavily associated, not only for its presence within the Wild Hunt, but also for the fact that the black dog is a form traditionally taken by the Old One in bestial manifestation, just as the black dog is also one of the manifold forms taken by the witch in travelling forth in spirit by night.

Within the magical rites and workings of the witch, the protective influences of the spirit hound and its ability to inspire fear and great dread, both have their uses. At times when danger threatens, of either a spiritual or mundane nature, the witch might perform a rite to call forth the protective presence of the Wisht Hounds. Such a rite may be performed to raise the hounds in protection about an individual, or a place to be warded by their influence.

It is, of course, important that the secret operations of witchcraft go unseen by prying eyes, and are guarded from possible intrusions and disruption. Where Craft meetings and workings are to take place in locations where night-time walkers are a possibility, the raising of the hounds might be incorporated into the Compass conjurations in order to guard and conceal the night's activities. In some witchcraft traditions, the summoning of the hounds is an established aspect of the Compass rite.

At times, when the source of danger or threat is known, or the originator of wrongdoing, mundane or magical, is identified, then the dark hounds of the hunt will be sent forth in a rite of 'turning'. The work of turning is a magical act, for which there are many traditional methods, of turning back all ill influence and directing it manifold unto the wrongdoer from whom it came.

Here shall be given both a rite of warding, and a rite of turning; both adaptable for various circumstances. The warding may be incorporated into the Compass or Castle rites previously given, in order to shield a rite or working from intrusion. If it is an individual who requires the influence of protection, or the turning away of ill-influence, then they will be made to stand in the centre of the Compass so that the appropriate rite may be performed about them. If it is a place that requires protection or a turning, then the rite should, as far as possible, encompass that place; be it a building or an area of land etc.

## A Call unto the Wisht Hounds

Have for this working the blackthorn staff, being naturally defensive in virtue, the lunar winding horn, a censer of coals, herbs of protective virtues to burn therein, and all else that may be required for any rites and workings to be done that night.

After the working ground has been cleared and the Circle marked upon the earth, the horn, censer and herbs shall be set at the North-West of the perimeter, and the place will be exorcised by whatever method is preferred. If this rite is being undertaken in order to bring protections upon a rite or working of the Craft, then it shall be preceded by the usual rites of the Castle, and the rite here given shall follow the conjurations of the Compass.

With the blackthorn staff in hand, the operator shall go to stand in the North-West, facing outward from the circle. The horn is taken up and these words are spoken:

*Ancient Lord of the Mound,*
*By blackthorn staff and hunting horn,*
*Let ye forth the faery Hounds,*
*Silent and of shadow-form.*

# THE DEVIL'S DOZEN

The herbs are cast upon the coals, and within the up-born smoke the horn is sounded thrice. The horn is replaced before the smouldering herbs and the conjuration is given in full, three times around the Compass bearing the blackthorn staff in the rightward direction:

*Ancient Lord of the Mound,*
*By blackthorn staff and hunting horn,*
*Let ye forth the faery Hounds,*
*Silent and of shadow-form.*
*By wandering moon and midnight skies,*
*Shadow Hounds and Spirits Grim,*
*Hear our call, awake, arise,*
*Pace the Round and ward the rim.*
*Forgather to the Compass-Round,*
*About the Circle now appear,*
*Prowl and guard the Castle's bound,*
*No foe nor stranger to come near.*
*About us draw the cloak of night,*
*Herein the power to increase,*
*Be all intrusion put to flight!*
*By Mercy, Justice, Truth and Peace.*

The burning censer, replenished with herbs, is then carried thrice about the Compass, again in a rightward direction. Where this rite is performed as part of a covine meet, it might be well employed as a mill chant, in further conjuration for the manifestation of the Spirit Hounds.

## A Rite of Turning

Have again for this rite the blackthorn staff, the horn, and a censer of burning coals. The herbs for burning shall be ones of a turning, exorcising virtue, and the iron knife shall also be present. The Circle having been marked, the horn, censer and knife, pointing outward, shall all be set at the perimeter in the direction of the wrongdoer or perpetrator of ill-influence. The herbs are cast upon the coals to burn, and the blackthorn staff is used to conjure a Compass of lifting and exorcism without words, three times around in the leftward direction. On the third casting, a banishing pentagram is conjured with the blackthorn staff at each of the cardinal directions, and stabbed through the centre with the point of the staff. The herbs are replenished upon the coals and the censer carried thrice, in the leftward direction. The censer is replaced at the circle's edge and the horn is taken up. The blackthorn staff is held aloft to point in the direction of the wrongdoer and, looking through the left eye, the operator gives the conjuration:

*By Old Herne and Gabriel,*
*Coal-black and eyes aflame,*
*I Conjure forth the Hounds of Hell,*
*Go forth in Old Dewer's Name!*
*The hunt begin by winding horn,*
*Stalk [name of wrongdoer] ever near,*
*The way be set by blasting thorn,*
*Each night to put her heart in fear.*
*Her evil back upon her go,*
*Baying Hounds about her turn,*
*Cursed be the wicked foe,*
*Her cruel heart to waste and burn!*
*Catch her thrice within thy glare,*
*I send ye forth by witch's rite,*
*By tooth and claw her heart to tear,*
*Hunt her now with turning spite!*
*So Shall it be!*

# THE WISHT HOUNDS

Still pointing with the blackthorn staff, and still looking through the left eye 'seeing' the wrongdoer, the horn is loudly sounded three times and the rite is done.

# The Light Betwixt
*Witch-fire & the Grand Array*

**W**idespread is the old witch tradition of the 'Devil's Devotional' at the rites of the witches' Sabbat. These rites, which might appear at first to be purely acts of homage by the assembled witches, have at their very heart the Old One and the primal fire of mystic luminosity.

Within such rites, this light is embodied within the Devil's candle or torch being held aloft by the Old One, or affixed between the twain horns of his head. In French witch lore he appears as the archetypal black goat-god of the witches bearing the candle betwixt his horns. At Scottish witch gatherings he appeared in the likeness of a man, or in therianthropic guise, bearing a candle in his hand, or the scene of the ceremony was illuminated by the lights of black tapers, such as in the witch rites said to have been conducted within North Berwick Church.

# THE DEVIL'S DOZEN

The pitch-black tapers of the Devil's devotional may be seen to be emblematic of various Craft tenets. The use of black pitch instead of the usual white wax may embody just one of numerous traditional acts of ritual 'inversion' employed upon our old friend; the transgressive path of 'return'. Exemplified also are the luminosity of power and spiritual gnosis concealed and to be found by the Wise within the mysteries of night, the Divine spark of creation born forth from the dark, and the bearer of that spark unto the blood of the Wise – the dark-guised bringer of light; the witches' god in whose image we may find such avatars as Lord Lucifer and the Goat Lord Azazel, the old sorcerer-farmer Cain and sorcerer-smith Tubal-Cain – Bearers all of the primal 'serpent blood'.

As the inheritance of the old serpent burns also in the 'faery blood' of the witch, the 'Devil's devotionals' are thus not merely ceremonial displays of homage, but potent rites of communion with the mystic light, exemplified in acts to be found within this profound aspect of the old Sabbat. The burning black tapers, described as being held by the witches in their worship of the 'Devil', were either lit by the witches themselves from the light held by the Old One, or the Old One himself would ceremonially kindle each of the witches tapers from his own flame. Herein the Wise may discern a ritual act of communion; a partaking of the mystic light of 'all-wisdom' and an affirmation of the inner fire of the witch. That the source and symbolic reification of this 'witch-fire' is acknowledged to be the Old One himself, may be affirmed in the returning of these tapers to the 'Devil' at the closing of the rite, as was said to occur in the meetings of witches in Somerset.

We might see further affirmation of the inner 'witch-fire' in its 'fanning', stirring and raising by the use of joyous acts such as feasting and ritual mill-dances, the music for which may very well be played by the 'Devil' himself, or else he might seek to stir up the power in his witches by use of the scourge to 'whip up' the dance.

Whilst the 'Devil's Devotional' may be most often thought of as occurring at witch gatherings, about the manifest appearance of the Old One (present perhaps in the masked and hide covered magister), it is of course a ritual that may be easily and potently employed in solitary circumstance. As is only traditional, the presence of the Old One may be represented by the phallic 'godstone', or perhaps such a rite may be performed around an ancient menhir, associated by some with the raising of the old serpent of the land, and thus the stirring and raising of the fire within the 'serpent-blood' of the witch.

There are of course other devices which may be employed by the Crafter for our purpose; such as the stang, horned animal skulls or the skull of a man. In the use of the latter, the 'cross-bones' are used within some Craft traditions to symbolize the Old One of the death mysteries, useful of course within concomitant rites and magical workings where his presence is called upon. For our present purpose however, the bones would be positioned un-crossed and 'open', for such is symbolic of life, creation, increase and thus suitable to the generative work of raising the inner flame. All such devices it must be remembered however are but vessels for the actual spiritual presence of the Old One himself, and where such symbols are employed, it is the work of the witch, by their focused will and acts of devotion, to evoke the manifest presence of the Old One, signs of which may arise in various phenomena, in or around the vessel, in the successful rite.

Here shall be given two rituals, both with the purpose of the old 'Devil's devotional', yet each entirely distinct in detail – one suitable for performance in solitary circumstance, and one which requires an assembly of Fellows of the Arte. The former version however may be adapted for a group circumstance should an assembly of Crafters wish to make use of it.

## A Devotional Conjuration of the Witch-Fire

As with most Craft rites and workings, it is better that this be performed outdoors, in the secret place, or perhaps some other suitable place of power. It might, however, be performed indoors at the hearth, perhaps in the sanctuary of the 'working room' if one is so fortunate.

Required for our rite is some suitable representation of the Old One; such as a pair of animal horns, or a horned animal skull, or a human skull, or a carved image of the witch-god, or a god-stone, or the forked staff, pitchfork or witch's stang. Greenery associated with the virtues of both fire/Mars and earth/Saturn, and suggestive of the goat-god of the sabbat must be gathered; branches of fir or pine and its cones, along with leafy tendrils of ivy are ideal and may be found throughout the year. Gather also and mix pine needles, mugwort and the dragon's blood resin. A black candle will be obtained and a vessel suitable to contain a small fire will be prepared. Have also your witch's blade, and the cup, filled with a good drink.

Prepare an altar for your rite; be it a suitable flat rock or the earth itself swept clear, or the hearth, or some suitable piece of furniture if the rite is to be worked indoors. Arrange upon this altar your greenery in the form of a large equilateral triangle, pointing east if the circumstance of the location permits. Within the upper point of this triangle is to be set the image of the Old One, and the black candle affixed upon it, or between the horns if the image has them. If this is not possible, place the candle behind the image, in a candlestick tall enough to allow the candle to stand above the image. Before the image place the fire vessel, and build within it the fuel for the fire; gorse/furze and sticks are suitable for an outdoor rite, but charcoals might preferably be employed indoors, or perhaps a smokeless fire of alcohol spirit. To the left of this vessel place the cup of drink, and to the right, the witch's iron blade.

Take up first the knife, and trace the working circle, preferably to encompass the triangle at its centre, and large enough for dances to be made within it. Conjure it thrice with the compass conjuration given previously in the rite of the Nowl:

*Thrice be conjured Compass Round,*
*Devil's Acre, Dancing Ground,*
*Marked and hallowed Castle moat,*
*Blessed field of the goat!*
*Meadow of the Hidden Flame,*
*Hallowed in the Horned One's Name!*

Replace the knife, kneel before the triangle of arte, and let one's focus fall upon the image of the Old One. Light the candle of the image of the Old One, and let deep and silent contemplation be upon the old god of the witches; the first witch, progenitor and forefather of witchcraft and bearer of the light betwixt. Here, one encounters the embodiment of mystery, the pathway between the worlds, the shadow cast by the light and the fertile darkness from which the light is born forth. Give the call:

*Old goat god of the Wise,*
*Horned initiator, and first born,*
*Of Serpent fire, awake, arise!*
*By iron blade, by bone and horn!*
*Forefather of the Secret Arte,*
*Keeper of the meadow's flame,*

*Beacon of the witch's heart,*
*Light the path that has no name.*
*O Bearer of the mystic light,*
*Come ye as the fire burns*
*By the secret ways of Night*
*The witches' mill about thee turns!*

Let these last few lines develop into a chant as one arises to circumambulate the compass; further conjuring forth, with absolute focus of will, the presence of the Old One upon the image:

*O Bearer of the mystic light,*
*Come ye as the fire burns*
*By the secret ways of Night*
*The witches' mill about thee turns!*
*Eko, eko Azazel,*
*Eko, eko Lumiel,*
*Eko, eko Tubelo,*
*Eko, Eko Cain!*

When the presence of the Old One is strongly felt, or signalled by phenomena, the mill dance is brought to a stop as one returns to settle before the triangle. Here, the fire vessel is to be kindled from the Old One's candle, and as it burns let the eye gaze deep into its flames as contemplative focus falls upon the inner fire. Let the conjuration be given:

*Behold my bones — the forge and hearth,*
*lanthorn of the Dragon's flame,*
*A lamp to light the crooked path,*
*In the old horned witch-god's name!*
*My brow ablaze with the mark,*
*Vessel of magic and fiery seed,*
*A Devil's candle in the dark,*
*Hallowed flame of magic deed.*
*Stir ye serpent in my heart,*
*Wax and quicken the old witch-fire,*
*Secret forge of witching-arte,*
*Be kindled, fed and fanned yet higher!*

Cast now the pine needles, mugwort and the dragon's blood resin into the flames in offering, and begin to breathe deep and slow, as the bellows unto the forge-fire, to fan the inner flame to yet greater brilliance. When thy very bones are felt to be reddened and ablaze with witch-fire, take up the iron blade in the right hand and hold it within the fiery vessel until its tip is also reddened and aglow. Then shall the drink-filled cup be taken up in the left hand to receive the knife, plunged into its sweet depths and hissing as the Old Serpent. Let this act be accompanied with the conjuration:

> *Well of the wise, bloody mirror of Cain,*
> *In the sign of the horned cross aglow,*
> *The witch-cup of old I raise again,*
> *By serpent above, within and below.*
> *By Wise-blood and Cunning blade,*
> *Reddened with the serpent-seed,*
> *The hallowed troth of old remade,*
> *Elphame's fire to ever feed.*
> *By witch-blood and the faery-sight*
> *I conjure, hood and hallow thee,*
> *Blaze ye, raize thee to thy height,*
> *Blessed, cursed, and cunning be!*

Offer first the hallowed drink back unto the fire, and unto the image of the Old One before imbibing from the cup yourself. Further dances and chants may be made to further raise the witch-fire before the rite is brought to a close.

## A Devotional Mass
## for
## Old Master Bucca

Here shall be given a devotional covine rite of communion with the Old One and the witch-fire, in which one Fellow of the companie, by use of the 'Devil's Grand Array' shall be present as a living representative and vessel for Old Master Bucca. Required for the 'Grand Array' is a mask or head-dress fashioned by use of animal horns. Further enhancements may be made by use of animal skins, hides and hair to cover as much of the body in bestial guise as imagination and availability of materials dictate. Required also for this role are the 'spirit whip' or 'Devil's scourge' and a fire torch. Have arranged at the altar the things for the rite; the communion things, and an incense containing much dragon's blood so as to be of power and potency. Have there also a black taper for each fellow present, a white cloth, and other enjoyable foods and drinks for feasting. the broom and sword will be crossed at the North-Eastern edge of the Compass. The Magister of the companie, or another chosen Fellow, will depart some way from the working area, with the bestial raiments, the scourge and the unlit torch, to assume the guise and make, by arte, his invocations of the Old Horned One. The choice of individual will be made in full mindfulness that to enter such possession, one requires the skills to return from it again.

The Fellows will gather wood to build a small fire at the centre of the working area, and will begin the rites of the Compass, omitting the lighting and blessing of the fire, and the making of devotions at the altar staff.

When the companie are ready to begin the mill, each will take up an unlit candle, and the Maid of the rite will give the call:

*Bucca, Bucca, Bucca!*
*Horned one, dark and fair,*
*shrine hearth and vessel of all dualities*
*conjoined.*
*We dedicate this rite unto thee!*
*Guide us upon the path of all wisdom,*

*by the light betwixt the horns.*
*Bucca Gwidder, Bucca Dhu,*
*Bucca dark and Bucca fair,*
*By snake, by toad, by crow, and by hare*
*We bid thee - draw near.*
*By the way-betwixt; draw with us here!*
*Come thou and bring forth the light*
*betwixt the horns,*
*The light that illumines the old path of the*
*Pellar Way.*
*So shall it be!*

The Mill will then begin, in the direction against the sun, with all making the whispered chant;

*Bucca Bucca Bucca,*
*Buckie Bwca Bugh,*
*Buckie Bwca Hu!*

During this Mill, each must have their mind and Will fixed firmly upon calling the presence of The Old One to the Circle's edge.

When the Old Horned Master arrives at the North-Eastern edge of the Compass, bearing the now burning torch in the left hand, and the scourge in the right, the Mill will stop. The Fellows will now arrange in horseshoe formation, facing the Old Master with the unlit fire in their midst. Each in turn will approach, dropping in obeisance to make devotion and to kiss the earth, before raising to a position of genuflection for their candle to be lit from the light of the Old One's torch before returning to their place in the horseshoe of Fellows.

The Old One will enter forth, into the centre of the Compass to light the fire by use of the burning torch, and the Fellows, with burning candles in hand, will now begin pacing the Mill and chanting, in the direction of the sun, around the Old One and the fire, to raise further the Old One's presence, the serpent and the witch-fire within:

*Bucca Bucca Bucca,*
*Buckie Bwca Bugh,*
*Buckie Bwca Hu!*

The Old Master will symbolically 'whip up' the dance with the scourge in an act of spiritual fertilisation and empowerment of the companie, and may himself wish to join the Mill, which will then become a wild dance. The Mill is stopped when the Old Master stands at the altar, facing in toward the fire, laying the scourge down and taking up his blade instead. Each Fellow in turn approaches again, in genuflection, to place their candle to either side of the Old Master and the altar. The last to do so is the Maid of the rite, who will then take up the cup of drink and bowl of bread. These she will place before the Old Master, before whom she kneels to bless the communion in the usual way, and will then hold aloft the cup for the Old Master to lower into the drink his blade, thus conveying something of his spirit, so that the Fellows may partake of it.

The 'Lamorna Toast' is given at the fire as a little of the drink is first offered unto it:

*Here's to the Devil with his wooden pick and shovel, digging tin by the bushel with his tail cocked up!*

The bread and drink is passed around the Compass to be partaken of, and the white cloth is laid upon the earth before the Old Master, there to be set pleasingly with the food and drink of the feast, which the whole Company shall enjoy with much music and merriment before performing their rites of closing.

# All is One
## Union with the Old One and the Spirit World

**ithin** our rites, thus far given within this book, the theme of union pervades. Rites of compact, dedication, drawing and raising the fire of the Old One within, and invoking communion at the crossing of the Ways; all have at their heart the goal of union.

Within the lore, traditions and history of witchcraft however, the old accounts of sexual coupling with the Devil represent perhaps the most potent symbolic act of mystical re-union with the witch-god, the spirit world and wild atavism.

The historical records of the witch-cult often relate that such unions marked a sealing of the rites of initiation and diabolic compact; a tradition reflected perhaps in the rites of sexual induction employed within the initiatory rites of some contemporary Old Craft groups.

# ALL IS ONE

Whilst such acts in history might more popularly be thought of as taking place between female witches and the Devil in full masculine manifestation, male witches were also able to enjoin in mystic union with the 'Devil', for within the mysteries of the Sabbat we find that the Old One is possessed of the ability to manifest in female form, or will preside jointly over the rites of the witches with his female counterpart; the Queen of the Sabbat or the Queen of Elphame with whom male witches might enjoin in sexual congress. Again, such lore may be found reflected within the practices of some Old Craft traditions where female and male witches undergo sexual induction through the Magister and Magistra respectively. It is also to be remembered that, in sacred transgression of societal 'normality', same sex couplings are also to be found in the old lore of the witches' Sabbat, no matter how aggressively adverse some modern expressions of the Craft have been to such things.

As with many of the rites and ways given within these pages, transgression, inversion and atavism are old and potent artes of the witch that open the way unto the path of return; the path of One and mystic re-union.

Of course, transgression is potently enshrined symbolically in the act of union with the Devil, who is the part man, part bestial rend betwixt the worlds of man, nature and spirit. Therefore ritual union with the Old One is also an embodiment of an immersive union with wild nature and the spirit world itself.

Mystical union with the witch-god, the spirit world and the begetting of spirits is also there to be discerned by the witch's eye in the old lore of 'diabolic marriages', illustrated in the old accounts of the Devil appearing before the lone witch in order to take her through an impromptu ceremony of marriage.

Intrinsic to old witch-magic is contact with the spirit world and a working relationship with the familiar spirit; a source of information, an aid to magic, and a provider of counsel and spiritual companionship.

# ALL IS ONE

These are the beliefs dearly held by many a traditionally inclined witch, such as the West Country cunning man Cecil H. Williamson, who have each had their rites and ways of enjoining with the Old One and the spirit world, many of which involve ordeals of surrender and solitude. Via such rites, the witch becomes the living vessel of spirit forces and enwraped in the loving potency of the Old One himself.

# THE DEVIL'S DOZEN

## The Rite of Union

The only impedimenta required for this rite are some means of marking a circle, five candles or lanterns, and a means to light them. A suitable incense may also be chosen.

Alone, the witch must venture forth at nightfall, to some remote and desolate place, be it within the depth of a tangled and wild wood, or some old, forgotten and lonesome country building, so long as the the place chosen shall be free of all human intrusions.

Upon reaching the place, the witch will undress, mark out the circle upon the earth making it large enough for the witch to lay within with arms and legs comfortably outstretched. The candles are then to be arranged and lit, or lanterns are used if the place is exposed to sufficient breeze to extinguish an unguarded candle flame. They are to be placed one a little away from where the witch's head shall lay, and the others a little away from the outstretched hands and feet. The incense, if such has been chosen, is also to be lit nearby.

So the witch shall now lay down, upon the earth, enveloped within the dark of night, illuminated only by the five little flickering lights. Motionless, naked and exposed, far from the 'world of Man'; a fear or panic may arise that intensifies one's awareness of the unseen and the unkown. To these things the witch must surrender herself and be open as she makes the call:

*Within the Circle of the Wise,*
*My body pledged upon the earth,*
*my heart to thine at the old cross lies,*
*An oath and offering for rebirth.*
*Spirit of the Wise and Ways-between,*
*Hear ye this night my call,*
*Shifting shades, and presences unseen,*
*Open within the Way 'twixt All!*
*A vessel I call till thou art come,*
*A living shrine enfleshed by Night,*
*To hold within the Light of One,*
*A lamp to take the Devil's Light!*
*Enjoin ye Old One here with me,*
*The witches' covenant to seal,*
*This house of flesh I give to thee,*

*Herein thy mystery to reveal.*
*My body to thy care and aid,*
*Essences of the night-side old,*
*power, silence and spirit pervade,*
*Against all adversity thy cloak enfold!*

And there shall the witch remain, until the first returning light of day, laying completely motionless. Within the circle of fragile, dancing lights revealing subtle and shifting forms amidst the dark of night, the witch's fear shall give way unto trance, by which the spirit body loosens from the physical and merges with the spirit of the night itself. Imbibing of the potent world of the unseen, a feeling of comfort and safety arises amidst the watchful spirit eyes of night. It is here that the other-world becomes an unquestionable reality, and in her entranced communion with the unseen, its spirit-forces are drawn forth and enjoin with her. As she makes her continuous and silent calls into the night, so shall the Old One come forth and enter into union with the witch, who now becomes a bride and priestess of the

# ALL IS ONE

Old One, mother of spirits and the living shrine, lamp and vessel for the powers, wisdom and light that are born from the mysteries of Night.

# Skin Turning
# &
# The Wild Hunt

In the midst of a clearing, deep in a tangled wood, a small fire burns; its light rhythmically concealed and revealed by shifting shadowy forms treading a circle about it. Through the glowing smoke, rising to the crossed tree branches above, one can discern another figure, stood before the illuminating fire at the circle's midst. A dark and mysterious therianthropic man-beast is he; crowned with horns and hairy with animal skins. Looking closer at the shadowy folk; hooded and cloaked, pacing their mesmerising mill about the man of horns, one can see that they too are part bestial in nature, as glimpses of their faces in the firelight reveal the countenances of animals and creatures familiar and unknown.

Such a scene could well describe a clandestine gathering of Old Craft practitioners in the present day, yet it may also be reminiscent of the old lore and trial accounts of historical witchcraft.

Whilst the Devil in manifestation would often reveal himself in the form of a man, he could also choose from an array of animal forms in which to present himself unto his witches. Old accounts of such appearances reveal his favourite animal forms to include a hound or wolf, toad, boar, horse, cat, bird (such as a crow), and of course horned animals such as a goat, bull or a stag.

Yet, as the very embodiment of the rend in the veil; the opener of the Way betwixt the 'world of men' and the path of reunification with the wild and with Spirit, the Old One would also reveal himself in a form betwixt man and beast. Early descriptions of the Devil's manifest image are of an explicitly therianthropic nature. In addition to it being generally agreed that his form was of a being like a man, yet unusually large and often black, he bore horns upon his head and was possessed of cloven hooves instead of human feet. He may also have hands that are taloned and hairy like the rest of his skin. His ears may be long and pointed, and his eyes frightfully large for a human and mysteriously aglow or fiery.

In addition to supernatural manifestations of the Devil, we may discern in the old witch trial accounts suggestions that a man of the companie, such as the witch-master or leader of the gathering, would take on the role of living representation and 'vessel' of the Old One whilst suitably guised, just as may occur in present day gatherings of the Old Craft.

In some trials, the accused witches described the Devil's voice as sounding strangely 'hollow', suggestive of speech from within the coverings of a mask and a headdress of horns and animal hides. His body has been described as feeling cold and hard to the touch, like a corpse, which is also suggestive of disguises employing animal leathers, pelts or hides.

# THE DEVIL'S DOZEN

Whether a spiritual manifestation, or an invoked presence within a Magister of the Arte Magical, the Old One is encountered as a mystical union of man, beast and spirit, and via the old dances of the Sabbat, he leads his witches upon a path of return unto the blessings of such a re-union within themselves.

Indeed, it is an ancient belief that witches are possessed of the ability to shift their physical forms into those of various animals. Covens might perform dances of ritual skin-turning, such as taking on the form of the hare to be pursued by the Devil in the form of the hound. Bestial forms were also widely believed to be employed by witches in their private works of maleficia; for many was the time the appearance of some ordinary creature would be taken to be a witch in disguise; out to work harm by magical means. The folklore of witchcraft is heavily laden with tales of some injury being inflicted upon the unfortunate creature, after which some lonely old woman, long suspected of witcherie, would be found in her home, bearing a corresponding wound upon her own body – proof positive of her guilt and her shape-shifting ways.

Witches and the Devil both were said to enjoin with shifting bestial shadowy forms in the Wild Hunt; travelling forth as the otherworldly spirit horde across the twilight landscape, chasing death into life and life into death at the old times when the ways betwixt the worlds are opened.

Within some branches of the Craft, the old artes of bestial guising and 'skin-turning' continue as part of a rich corpus of ritual inversion, sacred atavism and return. Herein, the witch becomes a bridge betwixt the worlds of man and wild animalistic nature; a sacred and magical act of possession and re-union in which the witch also becomes a vessel and vehicle of the presence, potency and mystery of the Old One himself; the ultimate embodiment of 'otherness'. Through such immersive acts of 'unreality', an opening of the way betwixt the worlds is conjured forth, aided by other ritual techniques of mystical return and inversion, such as the performance of the Sabbat dances 'against the sun' and/ or back-to-back. Otherworldly gnosis and the fire of witch-blood may by such artes be stirred, fanned and raised; led by the Old One himself upon the path of One.

Here shall be given two rites; the first being a solitary rite by which one may become a living representative and vessel for the Old One, wild 'otherness' and the animalistic atavism of sacred return via the artes of magical invocation and possession. Such may be viewed as an initiatic act of union and taking on the mantle of priesthood unto the Old One.

Second shall be presented a rite of the witch-companie; an invocation and enactment of the Wild Hunt' in ecstatic raising of one's hidden bestial natures and immersive union with the manifest landscape and the spirit world.

## The Assumption of the Horns

Required for this is some manner of taking on the appearance of the Old

One. Such may be devised in the form of a horned or antlered headdress or mask, and employing animal hides and hair, as well as greenery, to cover the face and as much of the body as available materials permit. Have also a lantern and a vessel of horn or antler within which to hold a mixture prepared of such oils as vetivert, patchiouli and pine in olive oil.

Go forth at the closing of the day unto some place; remote, wooded, wild and forgotten by man. There, at the falling of dusk's veil, begin to gather fallen twigs and other dried debris of the wood with which to build a small fire in the centre of your chosen place of working, and assemble your lantern, the oil and your materials of guising to the fire's north.

Cast off thy clothing, and the mask of civilised man, and, naked unto the spirits and presences of the wild and darkling wood, light thy lantern and lift the horn vessel of oil above its light, holding it unto the dark of the northward way; giving forth a wordless call of inner yearning and desire for the company of the Old One. Begin then the anointing

of the brow, the hands and the feet with
these words:

*Emen, hetan,*
*Emen, hetan,*
*In thy Name, Ancient One,*
*I am for thee, arise in me!*
*Behold thy vessel; the Devil anointed!*
*Emen, hetan,*
*Emen, hetan!*

Begin now to take up and adorn thy form
with the bestial mask, horns, hairs and
hides of witch-guising and Devilish skin-
turning whilst the charm is intoned:

*Old One; untamed and ever-wild,*
*Thy living vessel I bid ye fill,*
*Dark bearer of the light exiled,*
*The Hidden Way of One reveal!*
*Hairy, horned and hard of hoof,*
*Wild witch-god; awake, arise,*
*Sharp of claw and of tooth,*
*Enflamed about with witching guise!*
*Thy fire in my blood to burn,*
*Thy wisdom in my bones reside,*
*Thy spirit enfleshed, my skin to turn,*

# SKIN TURNING

*Enfolded in thy hoary hide!*
*So shall it be,*
*So shall it be,*
*So shall it be!*

Now in Grand Array, let the self and the Night merge as one, and by will and breath, fan to brilliance the fire of the Old One within. With this act, the lantern shall be taken to light the fire built at the clearing's centre. Speak these words and let blaze the fire of Ancient Providence:

*Raise ye forth O Serpent-fire,*
*Conjured in the Old One's Name!*
*Stir ye, burn ye, fan ye higher,*
*Potent be the Serpent-flame!*

Tread now a path of return, against the sun, about the fire. Let the presence of the Old One pervade thy being and permeate to thy very bones. Chant and tread onwards until all delineation between the self and the Old One is dissolved, and thereafter let the words of the chant transform into bestial primal calls or silence, and let thy treading about the fire and thy course be given over to wild leaps, crawls or stillness as the Spirit dictates.

*Bucca Bucca Bucca,*
*Buckie Bwca Bugh,*
*Buckie Bwca Hu!*

## An All Hallows' Rite of The Wild Hunt

For this rite, to be conducted around the time of Hallowe'en, wild woodland, or some remote and rocky heath are ideal landscapes. The presence of a crossable stream would present an ideal enhancement to the rite. Two circles are to be prepared; one to be a place of the Otherworld, and the other to be of the manifest world of the living – twin circles of the dead and the quick.

Within the circle of the dead, a simple fire is to be built at its centre, the broom is placed at the north-eastern edge and around the circle's edge are placed masks prepared by the each Fellow of the covine in atavistic animalistic forms of their own choosing and imagining. Also within this ring of masks, and to the north of the fire, is the horned mask or headdress of the Old One accompanied by the spirit whip and a winding horn, which is best made from the thigh bone of a man if the companie is possessed of such an item, yet one of animal horn will also serve the rite well. Herbs or incenses of spirit calling virtue should also be present there.

Within the circle of the quick, wood for a fire is also to be gathered and prepared at its centre. Over this the chitty irons are to be arranged and a cauldron suspended therefrom, filled with red wine, apples, honey, autumnal fruits and sprigs of thyme.

An altar is built in the north, bearing a human skull, the horn-cup, a censer and incense of enlivening and joyful virtue, all flanked by black candles, or lanterns if the winds of the chosen landscape will not allow the survival of a naked candle flame. Drums, pipes and other musical instruments are also to be arranged within this circle.

The covine assemble around the outside of the circle of the dead, in silent contemplation of the rite ahead, and in communion with the place and its spirit presences. The Lady of the rite is first to enter the circle by stepping, left foot first, across the broom – that most potent of witch symbols of passage to-and-fro the worlds.

The Lady is then to take up the broom, and sweep the circle against the sun; her act is a solemn inner conjuration, preparing the encompassed ground as a rend in the veil between the worlds of the quick and the dead.

The broom is replaced and the Master of the rite then enters the circle across the broom, left foot afore, and is followed by the covine in the same manner. The rites of the Compass shall be observed before all take up their respective masks and kneel about the fire, which has been kindled by the Master of the rite. Let all hold forth their mask, looking through its eyes filled with the illumination of the fire beyond. Let all regard their mask as at once a mirror unto the deepest and most ancient reaches of the self, and a window unto the mysteries, potencies and presences of the Other. Let this contemplation become unto the witch a profound communion; imbibing deeply of the experience and of the wild sounds and sensations of the nocturnal landscape beyond the circle's bounds. The Master of the rite takes on first the horned mask or headdress of the Old One, and sounds the horn before he delivers a conjuration of 'skin turning':

*Hearken to the Devil's Horn*
*Open ye the Ways within*
*Awake thy ancient shifting form*
*Conjure it forth and turn thy skin!*
*All unfathomable that has of ancient been*
*Deepest held and furthest set*
*By waking sleep and Midnight's dream*
*All potential that may be yet.*
*Arise ye unto Midnight's call*
*Dreaming beasts awaken en-fleshed*
*Thy myriad resurrections of ancient all*

*Spirit and mystery manifest.*
*By time betwixt and Midnight's tide*
*Rouse from the deep, the wild and hidden*
*By mirror-mask and witches' hide*
*By call of horn; summoned and bidden!*

The Old One sounds the horn again and approaches the fire at the circle's midst, as each of the covine take on their own masks to imbibe deeply and drowse 'mazed' in the arising of their primordial, bestial, and Otherworldly natures. Thus entranced and enchanted, let all give outer expression and manifestation unto their inner transformation via body and voice, as the Old One presides at the fireside amidst the rite, as the focal embodiment of the mystery of Otherness, partaken of by the covine of skin-turned witches; swaying, crawling and writhing, and letting forth the stirrings of bestial calls into the Night.

Three blasts of the huntsman's horn are given by the Old One to call forth the spirits and shades to arise and enjoin with companie, as the veil betwixt the worlds is parted amidst such an invocation of

Otherness, atavistic Return and the Wild
Hunt itself:

*Upon this night of Hallantide*
*The veil betwixt to rend and part*
*We conjure forth the Midnight ride*
*By Devil's Horn and witching Arte.*
*Spirits of old arise ye forth*
*Let quick and dead conjoin this night*
*By the way 'twixt West and North*
*Let begin the Elder Rite!*
*Spirits, beasts and ghostly rade*
*Open now the Way of the Dead*
*Wild horde of witch and shade*
*Open the Way that's Huntsman-led.*
*Cavalcade of Fellows all*
*Ride ye forth with Devil's speed*
*Ride ye forth at Midnight's call*
*By Night-Mare's hoof and spirit-steed.*
*By flight of moth by bat and owl,*
*By spirit path and old Corpse Way*
*By Hunter's horn and black hound's howl*
*By haunted track and ancient Ley.*
*Go ye forth in the Old One's Name*
*Throughout and about, without and within*
*By the light of the Devil's flame*
*Let the Wild Hunt begin!*

# THE DEVIL'S DOZEN

The horn is sounded by the Old One again, and the spirit whip is lashed about in the air as the covine arise to dance a mill around the fire, against the sun with wild bestial calls. The Old One joins the dance for a while, and sounds the horn again as he crosses the broom to lead the covine and spirit companie out of the circle to dance around its perimeter three times with the sun. The lady takes up the broom, the horn sounds again and the Old One leads the companie forth on their wild dance out into the night.

The horn continues to sound now and then, and the skin-turned witches leap and call as they travel forth with the ghostly horde. Death is thus chased into life in an act of union betwixt primordial spirit presences and the manifest living landscape; spirit and matter conjoin.

Eventually, the second circle, the circle of the quick, is approached by the covine. Upon arrival, the Old one leads the dance thrice about its perimeter with the sun, during which the Lady lays the broom at its north-western edge, a portal via which the spirit world may enter the manifest world. The Old One leads the companie over the broom into the circle, where the dance continues with the sun. The Lady takes up the drum to provide a driving beat unto the Mill, perhaps by using a human bone as a beater in accordance with one tradition, whilst the Old One breaks from the dance to approach the centre of the circle and kindle the fire; its flames arising to lick the old cauldron-pot hanging above it.

When the time is right, the Old One shall signal the Mill and its music to stop by raising his arms. He is then passed the skull of man which he shall hold aloft the fire whilst giving a call unto the spirits and beloved ancestors to enjoin with the covine's feasting and festivity:

*O Spirits unto life return*
*Arise ye from land's deep hollow*
*The old fire does smoke and burn*
*A beacon light we bid ye follow.*
*O Spirits to the Circle come*
*Enjoin our feast this Hallowe's Night*
*With us dance the Mill as One*

*About the fire burning bright.*
*Gather ye Old Ones, spirits and shades*
*Come ye to this hallowed ground*
*Unto the joyous rites here made*
*Dance and tread the Castle's Round.*
*By witches' dance and serpent's coil*
*Beloved dead we thee invoke*
*The witches pot to gently boil*
*Amidst the sweet and rising smoke.*
*O Spirit presences draw ye near*
*Voices whisper and visions show*
*In fire, incense and shadows appear,*
*All the witch would seek to kmow.*
*By skull and bones crossed we conjure thee*
*Come ye forth, so shall it be!*

The skull is replaced in the north and the Lady fills, stirs and tends the old pot as drumming and music are continued; the covine relaxing after their exhaustive night's dances. When it is ready, some of the content of the cauldron is ladled into the horn cup by the Lady. Together the Lady and the Old One bless the feast as the Master's blade is lowered into the cup with the conjuration:

# SKIN TURNING

*By the sign of the skull and Midnight's Host*
*All blessing 'pon our brew and bread*
*'twixt Blood And Spirit a troth an toast*
*To All as One; the Quick and Dead!*
*Under the Horns a blessed feast*
*Unto our merry companie;*
*Spirits, witches, shadow-beasts*
*Conjured, Hood and Hallowed Be!*

A little of the drink is offered first unto the spirits by being poured upon the earth before the skull and cross-bones, and then shared by the companie. Music, feasting and frolicking continue into the night, before the covine remove their masks; the spirits and atavistic presences are bid farewell and the rite closed.

# The Bucca Vessel
## A Rite of the Oracular Skull

**T**he skulls of man and beast have long been employed within both the folk-magical artes and the rites of the Craft. Animal skulls are possessed of a vast tradition of protective virtue within popular magic, such as the horse skull, which the Cunning Man Cecil Williamson tells us would encourage the spirit world to 'look kindly' upon the places in which they were kept. They might be hung upon walls or from roof timbers, and have been found secreted beneath floorboards.

The skull is very much an object of the 'Way Betwixt', being emblematic of death as well as the vessel of life and power. As such they have also long been associated with the 'threshold' places of the home, being affixed on or above doors, buried beneath the threshold or secreted within the chimney to ward off all intrusion; of both a mundane and a spirit-world nature.

As a fetish of power, life and spirit force, the human skull is central to many an old tradition of healing magic, whether the relic of a saint, or the 'unchurched' skull of some anonymous individual. They might simply be touched to confer the curative virtue, parts of them carried as 'pocket charms', or water drunk from their interior. Often the latter practice has been an ancient part of the healing rites associated with holy wells and sacred springs, making use also of the potent virtues of the living waters of the earth.

It is little wonder that the skull is a very traditional companion to the rites and workings of the 'old style' witch, who devotes their life and arte unto contact and communion with the silent and unseen world of spirit. As well as a symbol of death, the bones are all that are strong enough to remain, long after the rest of the body has returned unto the earth, and as such they are representative of spiritual strength and endurance, as well as the life force that they once contained, something of which is felt to linger within their hollow form. It is thus that, to the witch, the skull is the implement par excellence for contacting the presences of the spirit world.

We are also told by Cecil Williamson that it is the way of old style witches to create and lovingly maintain 'house shrines', central to which is often the human skull as the quintessential spirit house, into which kindly spirits are conjured to take up residence.

Witches' skull-shrines unto spirit presences were also however set up on the high and lonely moor land rocky crags, where contact with the spirit world was made all the easier by the isolation and numinous virtue of the landscape. One such skull, in the original collection of Cecil Williamson, is however not that of a human but of a ram; once the centre piece of a witches' shrine high on Bodmin Moor. Perhaps this skull and its shrine were dedicated unto contact with the spirit world via the agency of the very embodiment of the rend in the veil – the Old One himself?

Anciently regarded as the 'seat of the soul' and closest to the heavens, the head is by tradition heavily associated with contact with the divine. It is within the head, or before its physical sight, that spiritual vision occurs, and it is from the head that the breath issues and the words of power are uttered forth, associating the head with the divine breath and Word of Creation. Thus the skull is forever to the Wise a sacred vessel of divine power, inspiration, vision and spirit presence.

Within the witch cult we indeed find the skull often at the centre of its rites; perhaps in the human skull arranged as the shrine and altar of the Work, or the animal skull-topped staff or 'stang' forming the witch-altar and the 'gateway' betwixt the worlds. It is about these altars and their skulls that the witches work to conjure forth spirit presences and manifestations, or visitations from the Old One himself. Thus the skull remains to the witch a potent device of vision and reaching out to the experience of the Otherworldly.

## A Rite of the Bucca Vessel

The working here given describes the creation of a physical housing and spirit fetish for the Old One, here using his name as employed by my own companie; the Bucca, to be as a guiding lamp and an oracle of 'All-wisdom'. The skull of a horned animal or of a human must be obtained and will be most suitable. Cleanse and prepare the skull with any designs that please and suitably inspire the mind. Give the skull eyes of mirror set into a base such as wood or bees' wax that fill the eye sockets, for when the Wise gaze into the eyes of the Bucca, it is our goal to see our very own self in All-Wisdom.

When the skull is suitably prepared, take it to some place of power, at a time between times; at equinox, at dusk or at midnight. Set the skull to hang upon the staff, as the rider upon the mare and Odin upon the tree, in the midst of the working area facing south. Behind the skull place a crucible of coals and wort of northern virtue to burn therein, a vessel of spirit of myrrh and a crow feather. To the right of the skull place an iron vessel in which a small fire is built, and a vessel of oil of the virtue of witch-fire. Before the skull have a bowl of fragrant and pleasing herbs and quartz stones gathered from the ploughed fields. Have there also an oil pungent and earthy in nature. To the left of the skull have a cup of water drawn from a holy well, and a vessel of the oil of Camphor. Have with you also those things needed to perform the rites of communion.

Become, and work the rites of the Compass, conjuring the virtues of the Ways into the circle to cross where the skull stands at its midst in quintessence. Bucca's presence is called potently into the centre with the treading of the mill. When it is done, the assembled fellows, re-affirming the raising of the inner fire, will stand in silence around the compass, facing outwards to look upon the animate land and skies whilst seeking and feeling to perceive Bucca's presence at the Companie's midst.

When this presence is perceived, all shall turn to face the centre as one will step forward to take up the skull from the staff, holding it aloft to the sky, to 'see' the seven fires encircle it as they conjure:

*Bucca above,*
*By the blood tides of the moon,*

*By the seasons of the sun,*
*By the virtues of the fires of Nevek,*
*I conjure thee, I conjure thee, I conjure thee.*

The skull is then be passed to another, who will kneel and lower the skull to the ground, pressing upon it to 'feel' it sinking deep into the earth, into the self and into Annown:

*Bucca below,*
*By all that is hidden 'neath the cross of the Ways,*
*By the wisdom that has gone before and goes still within the Compass's Round,*
*By the transformations of Ankow,*
*I conjure thee, I conjure thee, I conjure thee.*

The skull is passed on, and with the back to the east, the skull is held aloft above the fire into which has been cast some dragon's blood resin:

*Bucca Rüth,*
*By forge and serpent,*
*By the fire of Cunning fanned by the breath,*
*By the blade of Desire that does send forth*

143

*Will, spirit and sprowl,*
*I conjure thee, I conjure thee, I conjure thee.*

The witch takes the skull unto their mouth and breathes for a while into it, an exchange thus fanning the fire within it and within the self. They will anoint the surface of the skull with the oil of fiery virtue using the little finger of the right hand and 'see' this oil feeding further the 'bone-fire' of the Bucca vessel.

It is passed on, and with the back to the south the witch will kneel and fill the cavity of the skull with the herbs and quartz stones, and there with the inner eye see the skull en-fleshed in the greenery and life of the season:

*Bucca Gwidder,*
*By the white bones of the land within which*
*the serpent coils,*
*By the mare with the season for her skin,*
*By hedge, hill, hollow and hag-way,*
*I conjure thee, I conjure thee, I conjure thee.*

The skull is anointed with the oil of earthly virtue, employing the thumb of the right hand.

# THE BUCCA VESSEL

The skull is passed on, and with back to the west the witch will kneel to anoint the skull with oil of Camphor, by the sinistral ring finger with the conjuration:

*Bucca Lōs,*
*By the seas of change,*
*By the well of vision, healing and transformation,*
*By the toad of influence,*
*I conjure thee, I conjure thee, I conjure thee.*

The vessel of water, drawn forth from a holy well, is taken up and the skull sprinkled lightly as the witch 'sees' it take the water deep within as the earth does take the rain, therein to flow like blood.

The skull is passed on, and with the back to the north the skull is held aloft over the smoking crucible and the conjuration is given:

*Bucca Dhu,*
*By the haunted door 'twixt the worlds,*
*By the mercurial winds of spirit,*
*By thy black storm-hounds and the midnight call of owl,*
*I conjure thee, I conjure thee, I conjure thee.*

# THE DEVIL'S DOZEN

The witch will take up now the crow feather, and with it coat the skull with the spirit of myrrh, as a haunted object of the death mysteries and initiatory revelation.

Each will now, in turn, hold the skull tenderly before them, and gaze into the eyes of the fetish before it is replaced upon the staff, when all shall begin a dextral round and speak unto it:

*Bucca, Bucca, Bucca!*
*Horned androgyne dark and fair,*
*Regis of the Wise,*
*Ancient One ever young,*
*Striker of terror in the hearts of all,*
*Tenderest lover and seducer of all,*
*Truth teller and deceiver of all,*
*Mirror twin, and shadow opposer of all,*
*Father, Mother, initiator and bringer of the crooked path unto the Cunning,*
*Trod in darkness and in light,*
*Blessed and accursed,*
*Behold this vessel of bone filled with thy spirit,*
*Bucca, Bucca, Bucca,*
*Quintessence of all nature,*
*In thee are all dualities conjoined and resolved,*

# THE BUCCA VESSEL

*By the light betwixt thy horns,*
*May thy children attain All-Wisdom!*
*So shall it be!*

The rite is concluded with the celebration of the communion. As an oracle of All-Wisdom, let the skull's presence within the Compass be an aid to all rites of divination and of spirit communion. When knowledge of something is needed, it is fitting for a witch to take the vessel at midnight to a remote stone stile within a hedge. There place the skull, and set upon it a single lit candle. Sit upon the stile and celebrate a simple communion in Bucca's name. The witch will then stare into the eyes of the fetish intently, and unwaveringly, no matter what distractions may occur, until an answer or wisdom has been received through voices in the sounds of the place, or in visions at the edge of the eye's perception.

# The Old Farmer

**A**gain we come to the old skull's focal centrality to the rites and magical artes of the witch. The foliate skull is richly emblematic of Cain – the Tiller, first farmer, first gardner, first magician, and of the Woodwose – the wild green spirit-man of the haunted primal forests, deeply associated also with the Faery King and the Wild Huntsman; his horn calling forth the powers and presences of the spirit-world and the wild to arise.

The 'Old Green One', or the 'Old Farmer' is thus patron, initiator, guide and teacher unto the 'Wort-Cunner' and witch whose arte and Craft employs the harvests of hedge, field, forest and heath for the making of plant charms and magical smokes, powders, oils, unguents and brews.

As with all the artes of witchcraft, such substances can be employed both to cure and to curse, and so, for the green witch, the foliate skull is emblematic of the 'double ways' of life and death. The Old Farmer shows in his countenance both the virid unfurlment of life and whitened bone of death, for he is both the reaper and the keeper life. Reddened with the rusts of Autumn is the land in its waning, and bare as the clean-picked bones of death in winter, yet its living spirit remains emblematically visible and kindled within the evergreens; serving a reminder of the verdancy to return in burgeoning potency through Spring into the zenith of Summer.

The foliate skull is also a potent Craft emblem of the mysteries of the Way of Return and re-union with the Other. The skull is, of course, the quintessential death emblem and of communion with the spirit world; its powers, presences and wisdom. The virid foliage represents the wild, the primal, the powerful and untamed. The old spirit of the hedge – bearer of working gifts unto the Craft of the green witch – is also the keeper of the Way between. The hedge is the ancient physical and metaphorical boundary;

delineating and separating the civility of 'the world of Man' from the semi-tamed cultivated land, and cultivation from the untamed and haunted wilderness beyond. The spirit of the hedge, as keeper of the Way, is also thus the beckoner unto the witch to follow across the stile and set upon the old path of Return unto the primal forests and gardens of the Other, and reunite with all that was lost in the great separation.

To wear greenery is to overtly state one's otherness from the 'civilised folk', to be wild untamed and powerful as the Old One's kin.

To the witch's eye, the virid foliate head represents a potent emblem of initiatic mysteries; of one consumed with primal and wild divine consciousness, power and inspiration. It is a vision also of spiritual fertility, potency and magical actuation.

I shall give here a witch-rite, initiatory in nature, for the Crafter who seeks to take on the old mantle of Verdelet, or Green-Cap (cape), to work the old Craft of the wort-cunner and hedge-doctor. It is a rite in which the initiate will set forth to commune with the Old Farmer, to burn bright with his virid fire and imbibe in divine inspiration of the potencies, wisdom and virtues of root, stem, leaf, bud, flower, fruit and seed.

## A Rite of the Green-Cap

The rite is here given as one worked by a companie of the Craft, yet, as always one may extemporise to adapt the rite for solitary enactment.

The Circle will be arranged with a fire in its centre, with the cauldron set to hang above. The altar will be arranged in the south, the direction of the fertile earth, and at the centre of this altar arrangement will be set the old skull. For this rite, the skull shall represent the Green Master – the Old God and Lord of the wildwood – the first farmer, teacher of the green witch's arte and keeper of all the gnosis of wort-cunning; the wisdom of trees, herbs, plants, seeds, resins, essences and all the verdant gifts of the land.

Encircling the skull shall be a necklace crafted of Oak, Ash and of Thorn, and placed nearby shall be a green cape; both being mantles and 'badges of office' for the covine's 'Green-Cap'.

The candidate for Green-Cap will have brought to the place the ingredients and things necessary for the preparation within the cauldron of some simple concoction of their choosing, which shall be for some general beneficial purpose. This shall be administered unto the covine as a token example of her or his Craft and Arte as a green witch.

All participating in this rite shall wear chaplets of gathered greenery, and shall bring with them unto the meeting bunches of various sweet smelling and potent herbs of the garden.

Following the rites of the Compass, let all stand about the central fire, each holding close their herbs; imbibing deeply upon their potent scent, and allowing the senses to draw deeply upon the potencies of the green.

The presiding witch shall then call:

*Green father,*
*Of thicket, field and hedge,*
*Lord of the verdant fires that in the*
*greenwood abide,*
*By all that grows forth, by seed, bulb, root*
*and spore from thy dark and fertile plot,*
*We Conjure thee, we conjure thee, we conjure*
*thee!*
*Be raised this night and fill thy bone graal*
*and skull-vessel!*
*Vivified by green-fire!*
*Elder of Gods!*
*Awake and arise, so shall it be!*

Those assembled shall each in turn now approach the altar, and offer up in dedication their herbs about the old skull. Then shall begin the treading of a dextral mill; each inwardly, by strength of will and fixedness of focus, conjuring forth the presence upon the skull; to see it aglow and enfleshed with living green fire.

When the presence is strongly felt, the round shall cease, and the candidate for

Green-Cap shall first approach the skull, and there, in dedication, offer up further herbs and replenish the incense resins upon the coals.

There shall the candidate stay, in inner communion with the Green Father; open as a vessel to be filled with his presence, wisdom and power.

When the candidate feels the time is right, s/he shall stand, and turn to face the centre of the circle. Two witches shall approach; one shall wrap about the candidate's shoulders the cloak of green, and the other shall place about their neck the necklace of Oak, Ash and Thorn. The presiding witch shall then say:

*Be thine own the wisdom, virtues and potencies of the green!*
*Be thine own the gifts of hedge, and hillside, meadow and heath, greenwood and darkest thicket!*
*For root and resin, bud and leaf, seed, flower, fruit and essence,*
*And all that is born forth of the earth,*
*Are the tools for the mastery of thy Arte and Green Craft!*

*For behold! Wort-Cunner and Green-Cap-witch thou art!*
*So shall it be!*

All repeat 'So shall it be!' and the new Green-Cap shall now step forth to work upon their preparation within the cauldron, whilst the covine treads a dextral mill; raising the green virtues within the Green-Cap and the preparation in progress within the cauldron.

When the preparation is ready, the Green-Cap will signal for the mill to stop by striking the cauldron thrice with the ladle, before blessing the cauldron's content as would be done that of the horn-cup. The presiding witch shall then bring forth the skull-cup for the Green-Cap to fill with the preparation and to first partake of it before it is shared by the gathered companie and the rite concluded.

## Other Books by Gemma Gary

Traditional Witchcaft – *A Cornish Book of Ways*
(Troy, 2008)

The Black Toad – *West Country Witchcraft &
Magic* (Troy, 2012)

The Charmer's Psalter (Troy, 2013)

Wisht Waters – *Aqueous Magica & the Cult of
Holy Wells* (Three Hands Press, 2014)

## As Contributor

Hoofprints in the Wildwood – *A Devotional for
the Horned Lord* (Richard Derks, 2011)

The Museum of Witchcraft – *A Magical History*
(The Occult Art Company, 2011)

The Long Hidden Friend (Troy, 2013)

Serpent Songs (Scarlet Imprint, 2013)

Hands of Apostasy – *Essays on Traditional
Witchcraft* (Three Hands Press, 2014)

# Bibliography

*Briggs, Robin. Witches & Neighbours. Fontana Press, 1997.*

*Brodie-Innes, J,W. The Devil's Mistress. Ramble House, 2006.*

*de Mattos Frisvold, Nicholaj. Craft of the Untamed. Mandrake, 2011.*

*Draco, Melusine. By Spellbook & Candle. Moon Books, 2012.*

*Duffy, Martin. 'The Shod Stang'. The Cauldron No. 131.*

*Ginzburg, Carlo. Ecstasies – Deciphering the Witches' Sabbath. Hutchinson Radius, 1990.*

*Hole, Christina. Witchcraft in Britain. Granada, 1979.*

*Howard, Michael. Children of Cain. Three Hands Press, 2011.*

*Liber Nox. Skylight Press, 2014.*

*The Book of Fallen Angels. Capall Bann, 2004.*

*& Jackson, Nigel. The Pillars of Tubal-Cain. Capall Bann, 2000.*

*Welsh Witches & Wizards. Three Hands Press, 2009.*

*West Country Witches. Three Hands Press, 2010.*

*Huson, Paul. Mastering Witchcraft. G.P. Putnam's Sons, 1970.*

*Jackson, Nigel. Call of the Horned Piper. Capall Bann, 1994.*

   *Masks of Misrule. Capall Bann, 1996.*

*Liddell, W.E. & Howard, Michael. The Pickingill Papers. Capall Bann, 1994.*

*Lucas, Theresa, A. 'The Black Faced God'. The Cauldron No. 142.*

*Maxwell-Stuart, P.G. Witchcraft – A History. Tempus, 2000.*

*Patterson, Steve. Williamson, Cecil. H. Cecil Williamson's Book of Witchcraft. Troy Books, 2014.*

*Pearson, Nigel. Treading the Mill. Capall Bann, 2007.*

*Pickering, David. Dictionary of Witchcraft. Brockhampton Press, 1996.*

*Wilby, Emma. Cunning Folk & Familiar Spirits. Sussex Academic Press, 2005.*

   *The Visions of Isobel Gowdie. Sussex Academic Press, 2010.*